BEAT 'EM BUCS
The 1960 Pittsburgh Pirates

GEORGE R. SKORNICKEL

PublishAmerica
Baltimore

© 2010 by George R. Skornickel.

All rights reserved. No part of this book may be reproduced, stored in a retrieval system or transmitted in any form or by any means without the prior written permission of the publishers, except by a reviewer who may quote brief passages in a review to be printed in a newspaper, magazine or journal.

First printing

PublishAmerica has allowed this work to remain exactly as the author intended, verbatim, without editorial input.

Hardcover 978-1-4512-0828-3
Softcover 978-1-4512-0848-1
PUBLISHED BY PUBLISHAMERICA, LLLP
www.publishamerica.com
Baltimore

Printed in the United States of America

This book is dedicated to:

My wife, Kathy, for her constant support and encouragement, my daughter, Kia, for helping me to remember the joy of shelling peanuts and rooting for the Bucs, my mother, who taught me the art of autograph collecting, and to the men of the 1960 Pirates for giving me a lifetime of special memories.

"A champion is not always a consistent winner.
He may have been a one-time loser who would not quit."

—Vernon Law

TABLE OF CONTENTS

INTRODUCTION 7

CHAPTER 1 13

CHAPTER 2
PRELUDE TO A CHAMPIONSHIP:
   THE TRADES 18

CHAPTER 3
1959: ElRoy Face: The Baron of the Bullpen and Harvey Haddix:
   Almost Perfect 22

CHAPTER 4
THE 1960 SEASON 33

CHAPTER 5
1960 WORLD SERIES: GAME 1 39

CHAPTER 6
1960 WORLD SERIES: GAME 2 52

CHAPTER 7
1960 WORLD SERIES: GAME 3 65

CHAPTER 8
1960 WORLD SERIES: GAME 4 77

CHAPTER 9
1960 WORLD SERIES: GAME 5 101

CHAPTER 10
1960 WORLD SERIES: GAME 6 113

CHAPTER 11
1960 WORLD SERIES: GAME 7 123

CHAPTER 12
We Had 'em All The Way: Fan and Player Reactions 139

CHAPTER 13
DID THE BETTER TEAM LOSE? 144

CHAPTER 14
WE STILL HONOR AND REMEMBER:
  THE MAZEROSKI WALL 152

AFTERWORD 156

APPENDIX A
1960 Pittsburgh Pirate Player Profiles/Statistics 158

APPENDIX B
1960 League Leaders 194

BIBLIOGRAPHY 198

INTRODUCTION

As a young boy growing up on the North Side of Pittsburgh, I had many opportunities to attend Pirate games at Forbes Field. I would catch the red and white 77/54 streetcar and take the rattling ride to Oakland. Once there, I would usually stop at Gus Millers' newsstand for a copy of the latest issue of *The Sporting News*, then cross the street to Weinstein's for a kosher corned beef sandwich, which I probably would eat sometime around the fourth inning. I remember distinctly the paper placemats the restaurant used during the 1960 season. They had a large picture of the team and the battle cry of "Beat 'em Bucs." From there it was just a short walk to the main gates of Forbes Field where there was always a great amount of activity. Just a few feet from the entrance was the Home Plate Café, which was actually shaped like home plate. Today the building serves as an intimate little theater used by the University of Pittsburgh. Tom and Jerry's was a long narrow building famous for its hot dogs and Cokes. Occasionally you would hear Benny Benack and his Iron City Six playing the Pirate fight song: "The Bucs Are Goin' All The Way." Going to Forbes Field for a game was an event even before you got through the gate.

My most vivid memory of Forbes Field centers around a

baseball which currently sits on the desk in my study. It happened in 1960 when I was thirteen years old. I had gotten to the ballpark early (I was usually the first one to shoot under the metal garage-type doors that sealed off the entrances) and had stationed myself at the railing next to the Pirate dug-out. At Forbes Field the seats were close enough to the field so that if you got there early and found a good place at the railing, you could actually smell the tobacco juice and the sweat. Slowly, in pairs and small groups, the Pirates began to take the field for fielding practice. All it took in those days to get an autograph was a degree of politeness and a good spot at the rail. Just about all of the players would wave, say a few words, or stop to sign an autograph.

Having had a lot of experience "at the rail," I always had a program and my trusty Louisville Slugger bat shaped pen. Finally, my favorite player, Roberto Clemente, appeared. He motioned to Joe Christopher and they began catching warm-up tosses along the first base line. I was always fascinated with the effortless way Clemente always seemed to catch and throw the ball. His side-armed, almost under-handed tosses to Christopher smacked into the glove with a surprising amount of force. Mustering up all the courage I could, I yelled, "Roberto, Roberto." He looked over, gave a sort of half smile, and waved his glove. I was kind of a regular, so there was a degree of familiarity in his response. After a few more tosses I yelled, "Roberto. Can I have the ball when you're done?" His response was an almost unnoticed nod of his head. I was thrilled. I had gotten his autograph on many occasions, and had several opportunities to talk to him, but now I was going to get a thirteen year-old version of the Holy Grail - an official Warren Giles National League baseball. Knowing I was going to get the ball when the bell rang to end warm-ups, I moved back a few rows to watch the players. After what seemed like an eternity, the bell rang and the players started to head for the dug-out. Clemente grabbed the final toss from Christopher and looked toward the seats. We made eye contact and he tossed the ball in the air in my direction. The next thing I knew I was hit from behind and found myself heading head-first for one of the blue wooden seats. Luckily I caught my balance and turned around just in time to see a heavy-set man of about forty grabbing the ball. With tears in my eyes I began walking to my seat. Suddenly I heard a loud voice booming the words, "Give the kid the ball!" I turned toward the rail and saw Clemente with one foot on the railing ready to leap over. The man who had knocked me flying suddenly appeared, stuffed the ball in my hand, muttered something I couldn't understand, and walked away. Looking at the ball I saw the words Rawlings, Warren Giles, and National League. I had my treasure. I was so excited I almost didn't hear Clemente yell, "Kid. Are you alright?" He still had his foot on the rail. He also had a look of deep concern on his face. All I could do was shake my head up and down. He stepped back onto the field and motioned with his mitt for me to come down to the rail. On shaky legs I slowly approached him. "Are you sure you're O.K?" he asked again. Once more I shook my head. "Got a pen?" I reached into the back pocket of my jeans and pulled out my trusty Louisville Slugger pen. Taking the pen from me with one hand, and the ball with the other, he signed the ball with his distinctive autograph. He smiled while handing me the ball and pen. "You be careful now," he said as he began to walk toward the dug-out. "Thanks, Roberto," I yelled. He stopped, smiled, waved with his glove, and disappeared into the dug-out.

Later that afternoon I sat in the front row of the right field stands cheering every time Clemente came into position, caught a fly, or batted, the ball bulging in the pocket of my jeans. I can't remember if we won or lost, but when I think of Forbes Field with its huge green scoreboard with its Longines clock and the scorekeeper looking out through its' openings, the batting cage stored in centerfield because few if any batters could hit a ball that far, the red brick with the ivy, and as Yankee Tony Kubek would find out, the rock-hard infield, I always remember the day in that 1960 season when Clemente signed a practice ball for me.

The 1960 baseball season was memorable to Pittsburgh Pirate fans and baseball fans in general for many reasons. It was the last year that both the National and American Leagues were composed of eight teams each playing a 154 game schedule. Faced with the threat of a proposed rival Continental League by Branch Rickey Jr., the American League approved the transfer of the Washington Senators franchise to Minneapolis-St. Paul, creating the Twins, and in 1961 would give Washington a "new" Senators team, while adding the Los Angeles Angels, making the American League the first Major League loop to have that many teams since 1899. Expansion would continue with the New York Mets and Houston Colt '45s joining the National League in 1962. White Sox owner Bill Veek became the first owner to put names on his team's uniforms while adding an exploding scoreboard to Cominsky Park.

Roger Maris became a Yankee while also winning the American League MVP award. It was the first time in major league history that both batting leaders hit under .330, and the first time in Major League history, except for the war-shortened seasons that no one in either league made more than 190 hits. Dick Groat of the Pirates finished at .325 while winning the National League MVP award, and Pete Runnels of the Red Sox hit .320. Frank Lary of Detroit topped the American League with 15 complete games, the lowest total to that juncture ever to lead a league, while Lindy McDaniel of the St. Louis Cardinals set a new Major League record with 26 saves. Other records set that year included the New York Yankees allowing only 2.83 runs per game on the road, while the Cleveland Indians scored a record low 2.65 runs per game on their road trips. Philadelphia Phillie Pancho Herrera set a National league record for striking out 136 times, the most ever in a 154 game season.

It was also the year that Ted Williams decided to call it a day and retire from the confines of historic Fenway Park home of the "green monster", Fenway's towering left field wall has outlasted Williams by forty years, hosting the 1999 All Star Game and still considered one of the grand old ladies of the game. Many of her sisters have disappeared, including Forbes Field, home of the Pittsburgh Pirates from 1909 to 1970. Forbes Fields' modern replacement, Three Rivers Stadium (Usually referred to as a "great football stadium"), was to be replaced by PNC Park whose towering light towers and pale yellow brick facade are strikingly reminiscent of old Forbes.

Forbes Field may be gone, but the memory of 1960, the year that the Pittsburgh Pirates, a loveable group of over-achievers who specialized in come from behind victories, outlasted the mighty New York Yankees in seven games to take the world championship for the first time in thirty-five years, is still fresh in the minds of those old enough to have experienced it firsthand. Behind the Cy Young award winning arm of Vernon Law, Dick Groat's league leading .325 average, and a propensity for winning games in the last at bat with a different hero every game, the Pirates of 1960 continue to fascinate Pittsburgh baseball fans. Although Pirate teams later won World Championships in 1971 and 1979, fan support for the heroes of 1960 is far more visible. Fans still travel to the remaining section of Forbes Fields' center field wall in Oakland every October 13th to listen to a tape of the deciding seventh game of the World Series, and every year they erupt in joyous celebration when they hear the call of Bill Mazeroski's dramatic bottom of the ninth home run. Not many people seem to talk about where they were when the Pirates won the final and deciding games in 1971 and 1979, but just ask someone where they were and what they were doing on September 13, 1960, and you'll not only get an answer, you will more than likely get a story that has become a very special part of their life.

The men of the 1960 Pittsburgh Pirates will remain forever young in our memories. Hal Smith being greeted at home plate after his seventh game home run, Gino Cimoli's cry of, "They set all the records, but we won the game!" in the victorious locker room, Mazeroski rounding the bases with the excitement of a Little Leaguer, ElRoy Face striding confidently to the mound, and Roberto Clemente firing the ball to the infield are images that will always be with us, along with announcer Bob Prince's, "We had 'em all the way!"

It is with gratitude for these wonderful memories that this book is written.

Chapter 1
The Impossible Pirates

The 1960 Pittsburgh Pirates did not exactly impress anyone in spring training.

Of the twenty-six baseball writers asked to select the order of finish in the major leagues by *The Sporting News*, only three picked the Pirates to meet the Yankees in the World Series.

Eight other writers went against the trend and picked the Pirates to win out in the National League.

Sixty-five others cast their vote for the Yankees, but were surprised by the Pirates.

Only one of the writers who picked the Pirates was a National League writer. Philip Grabowski of the *Post Gazette* picked his local boys to meet the Yankees.

Murry Kramer of the *Boston Record* and Merrell Whillesey of the *Washington Star* were the American League writers who hit both champions in their choice made at spring training.

Regardless of their showing before the season, manager Danny Murtaugh insisted that the Pirates won the pennant in spring training. Everyone had come into camp at Ft. Myers, Florida so full of energy and spirit you would have thought it was opening day. Feeling that he should reserve some of that spirit for when the games counted, Murtaugh cut the veterans' time in the batting cage in half. Murtaugh admitted that the players pouted, but when the season started they were like lions let out of a cage.

In a Pirate press release dated February 4, 1960, Murtaugh had the following comments about his soon to be championship team:

"Last year the Pirates had what I thought were two main weaknesses - the lack of another long ball hitter to go along with Dick Stuart, and the lack of a right-handed offensive catcher. We still haven't got the long ball hitter but we feel that we have acquired a good offensive catcher in the person of Hal Smith - .288 with Kansas City last year.

"Balance is the strong point of the 1960 Pirates. When all our ballplayers are playing to their potential, we do not have an outstanding weakness in our line-up. As our team now stands, we have a very good defense, adequate team speed, and a pretty good hitting team."

I do believe the Pirates will be stronger than last year, not only because of the trades we made but because I believe that several fellows on our team who had bad years last season will be much improved this year."

There are quite a few ball clubs in our league that must be considered 'teams to beat.' Naturally Los Angeles, the defending champion, is one of them. Milwaukee is always a powerhouse. Right now I consider the Giants as possibly the one team that could run away with the pennant because they acquired a lot of help in the department that I thought they showed some weakness in last year, namely pitching. In getting those two pitchers (Billy O'Dell and Billy Loes from Baltimore,) they don't give up too much to weaken their own ball club. I also feel that due to the closeness of all the teams in the National League in strength that if any one club can unexpectedly get two or three key players having a good year, they could win the pennant."

"We in the Pirates' organization feel that if all the boys on last year's ball club who had what we consider under-par years (Bob Friend, Bob Skinner, Dick Groat, Bill Mazeroski, Bill Virdon, George Witt) can play up to what they have played before, we must be considered as having a fighting chance for the pennant."

"If I had to pick rookies who I thought would make our club right now before Spring Training starts, I'd have to name left-handed pitcher Joe Gibbon, who pitched for Columbus last year and is training with us even though he's still on Columbus' roster, and right-hand pitcher Jim Umbright, who joined us at the close of the Pacific Coast League season last year after having starred at Salt Lake City."

Let's look at each player Murtaugh mentioned individuals and see how prophetic Murtaugh was.

HAL SMITH

On December 15, 1959 Ken Hamlin and Dick Hall were traded to Kansas City for Hal Smith.

Smith's stats in Kansas City: 108 AB, 84 H, 5 HR,
31 RBI, .288 BA
At Pittsburgh
77 AB, 76 H, 11 HR
45 RBI, .295 BA

His first two hits in the National League were doubles, and the next two were home runs. He had 20 RBIs on his first 21 hits, and 30 RBIs in his first 40 hits, 22 of which were for extra bases.

Also remember it was Smith's 8th inning home run in the 7th game of the World Series which gave the Pirates a 9-7 lead over the Yankees and set the stage for Maz in the 9th.

BOB FRIEND

The Pirates' player representative and ace right-hander came back from a miserable 1959 season to win the National League's "Comeback of the Year" for 1960.

In 1959 had: 35 G, 7 CG, W 8, L 19, 104 K, 2 SO,
4.02 E.R.A.

1060: 38 G, 16 CG, W 18, L 12, 183 K, 4 SO, 3.00 E.R.A.

Of Bob's 12 losses, 2 were by 1 run margins, 5 by 2 run margins, and 1 by a 3 run margin, so his record could have easily been even more impressive.

BOB SKINNER

The National League's starting left fielder in the mid-season All-Star game, Skinner had one of his best years in 1960.

His 145 games, 571 at bats, 15 home runs, and 86 RBIs were all career highs for him.

He began the season by hitting safely in the first 9 games. He had an 11 game hitting streak, two other nine game streaks, four eight gamers, two seven gamers, and one of six games.

His longest slumps of 1960 were of three game duration - once in June and again in August.

Bob jammed his thumb in the first game of the World Series and sat out the next five, returning to the lineup only in the final game. But in that vital 8th inning of the 7th game, he laid down a perfect bunt to advance Bill Virdon and Dick Groat.

BILL VIRDON

Virdon's stats stayed virtually the same from '59 to '60, but his average did jump from .254 to .264.

It was his fielding that mattered.

Virdon played an important role in the 4th Series game both offensively and defensively. Trailing 1-0, the Pirates did all their scoring in the 5th inning. Pitcher Vern Law singled home the first run to tie the score and then Virdon followed with a single to score two more and put the Bucs ahead, 3-1. The Yankees came back, however, and with the tying and lead runners on in the New York half of the 7th, Cerv hit a long fly to right-center which seemed headed for the bleachers until Virdon made a leaping, tumbling catch of the ball to stop the rally. Virdon made several equally brilliant catches in the Series but none carried the significance of the one in the 4th game.

And remember, it was Bill's ground ball to Kubek's throat that set up the Bucs amazing 8th inning rally!

DICK GROAT

Groat merely won the batting title and the M.V.P. award in 1960.

His average jumped from .275 to a league-leading .325. Hits from 163 to 186. He was at the .300 mark or above all but 5 days of the season.

BILL MAZEROSKI

Maz raised his average from .241 in 1959 to .273 in '60. RBIs were up from 59 to 64, hits from 119 to 147.

And, oh yeah, he hit the game winning home run in the 7th game of the Series to win the World Championship.

The only player mentioned by Murtaugh that did not have a better season in '60 was George Witt, his limited use both years makes a comparison hardly worth the effort.

When Danny looked into his crystal ball before the 1960 season he had a pretty clear view. Not only did those players do a lot to win the National League pennant, but a look at the highlight film shows some interesting Series action too. He was right on the mark!

CHAPTER 2
PRELUDE TO A CHAMPIONSHIP: THE TRADES

The climb to the top in of the National League in 1960 was a long and hard one for the Pittsburgh Pirates. In 1952 they had finished last in the League with a 42 - 112 record, earning them the title as one of the worst teams in baseball history. Nothing changes over the next three years as the Pirates laid permanent claim on last place with records of 50 - 104 in 1953, 53 - 101 in 1954 and 60 - 94 in 1955. They then proceeded to move up a notch in 1956, relinquishing last place to the Chicago Cubs, but then tied the same Cubs for seventh in 1957, which was still virtually the same as last place.

During those dismal years, however, General Manager Branch Rickey had assembled a group of players who were to become the nucleus of the 1960 championship team. Rickey had signed All American basketball player Dick Groat out of Duke in 1952. Rickey had seen Groat at a try-out and was so impressed that Dick came to the Pirates and the major leagues without ever having played one game of minor league ball.

In 1954, at a pre-spring training camp, Rickey observed seven shortstops taking part in fielding drills. One of the shortstops was a young player named William Stanley Mazeroski. When Maz took his turn at second base, Rickey was impressed with his quickness, agility, and the ability to throw without cocking his arm. Mazeroski later taught himself not to catch the ball in the pocket of his glove, but rather to deflect it off the heel into his throwing hand in the same motion, then throw to first.

The spring of 1954 was also when Rickey decided that pitcher ElRoy Face need more in his repertoire than a fastball and a curve to be successful in the major leagues. During spring training at the Pirate camp in Fort Pierce, Florida, Face saw veteran Joe Page throwing a forkball. He taught himself the pitch, and the rest is legend. He used the pitch to become one of the best relief pitchers in baseball.

Rickey and the Pirates also did a nice job of mining diamonds from the Brooklyn Dodger mines. As the former Dodger General Manager, Rickey knew Brooklyn was attempting to hide a talented Puerto Rican outfielder on their Montreal farm team. Knowing that, Rickey drafted Roberto Clemente for the Pirates. Five years later Clemente was an All Star batting .314.

The rebuilding of the Pirates reached another level in 1955 when Joe L. Brown, son of comedian Joe E. Brown, was hired to replace Branch Rickey as general manager. Brown had left UCLA in 1939 to enter professional baseball as an assistant business manager of Class D Lubbock. He later worked with clubs in Waterloo, Hollywood, Zanesville and Waco before finally making the front office at New Orleans. He also managed to serve three and a half years in the U. S. Army Air Force during World War II. Coming in to fill Branch Rickey's shoes was a big job, but Brown was about to show he was also a shrewd acquirer of talented and key players.

Brown's first acquisition which continued to build the core of the 1960 championship team was 1955 National League Rookie of the Year Bill Virdon whom he received from St. Louis in 1956 in exchange for Bobby DelGreco and Dick Littlefield. Virdon's speed and agility were well suited to the spacious confines of Forbes Field's centerfield. He was later to showcase his abilities on the field in World Series play in both Pittsburgh and New York.

In 1958, Brown traded Johnny O'Brien and Gene Freese to the St. Louis for Dick Schofield. Schofield was to become a vital cog in the '60 machine when he filled in for Dick Groat after Groat's wrist was broken by a pitch from Milwaukee's Lew Burdette on September 6th. Schofield responded to the challenge by hitting at a .368 clip.

At the time, one of Joe Brown's most questionable moves was drafting Rocky Nelson from Toronto at the 1958 Winter Baseball Meetings. Chub Feeny, general manager of the San Francisco Giants was said to have asked Brown if he meant "Ricky" Nelson, a popular rock and roll singer of the time. Brown was to have the last laugh when Nelson came through with a home run in the crucial 7th game of the 1960 World Series.

The most controversial trade of Brown's career occurred on January 31, 1959, when he traded Jim Pendleton, Whammy Douglas, Johnny Powers and home run hitting Frank Thomas to the Cincinnati Reds for pitcher Harvey Haddix, catcher Smoky Burgess and third baseman Don Hoak. In retrospect this was arguably the best deal Brown ever made. But at the time, Brown suffered the wrath of the Pirate fans for trading away a hometown hero who was hitting home runs in the tradition of Ralph Kiner. The three former Reds, however, proved to be the final pieces in the 1960 puzzle.

Another "almost" trade involving the future 1960 American and National League Most Valuable Players could have made the 1960 season even more interesting.

Pirate shortstop Dick Groat, who would go on in 1960 to win the National League batting title and the Most Valuable Player Award, came with minutes of becoming a Kansas City Athletic at the Major League's 1959 winter meetings in Miami.

The Pirates and the Athletics were discussing a multi-player deal centering around outfielder Roger Maris of the A's and Pittsburgh's Dick Groat, when Arnold Johnson, owner of the A's asked Pirate General Manager Joe L. Brown and field manager Danny Murtaugh to step out of the room.

Johnson had let it be known prior to the meetings that Maris was available. George Weiss, General Manager of the Yankees, wanted Maris, but Weiss was tired of the A's being referred to as the Yankees' farm club. Over the years the Yankees had acquired a large number of players through deals with the A's.

Brown and Murtaugh also expressed interest in Maris. They had discussed it and were ready to deal. Brown offered his package and the A's indicated agreement. It was then that he asked Brown and Murtaugh to step out for a moment so that Johnson and his aides could have a few private moments for final deliberation.

Brown could see that Murtaugh was upset. When asked what was wrong, he indicated that he wasn't sure it was a good deal. Murtaugh felt Dick Groat was the man holding the team together.

Brown and Murtaugh never returned to the meeting in Johnson's suite. They rode the elevator to the lobby where Joe Brown informed Johnson on a house phone that the deal was off.

Later, on December 11, 1959, Roger Maris was dealt with Joe DeMaestri to the New York Yankees for Hank Bauer, Don Larsen, Norm Siebern, and Marv Thoneberry.

A lot has been said and written about the trade that brought Don Hoak, Smoky Burgess, and Harvey Haddix to the Pirates from the Reds, but perhaps just as important to the success of the team in 1960 was the trade in 1959 that didn't happen.

CHAPTER 3
1959: ElRoy Face: The Baron of the Bullpen and Harvey Haddix: Almost Perfect

The 1959 season prepared the Pirate fans for the excitement of 1960 with two events that are a very important part of Pittsburgh Pirate history.

On the night of May 26, 1959, in Milwaukee's County Stadium, Harvey "the kitten" Haddix turned in one of the greatest pitching performances in the history of baseball. Haddix pitched perfect baseball for 12 innings, retiring the first 36 batters he faced, before the Milwaukee Braves scored on an error, a sacrifice, an intentional walk, and a home run, that later was ruled a double, defeating the Pirates 1 to 0, in the thirteenth inning on just one hit.

The Pirates managed 12 singles off Brave starter Lew Burdette, but could not score to preserve Haddix's masterpiece.

Haddix had started the day troubled by a cold. He got up at 7 o'clock to get to the airport in Pittsburgh in time for the 10 o'clock flight to Milwaukee. Arriving in Milwaukee around noon, he headed straight for bed in the Schroder Hotel and slept until 4. He then got up, ate a steak, and came to the park on the team bus.

He later told reporters that when he warmed up he just didn't feel well. He had been fighting off a cold and just figured to try to do his best.

True to tradition, the Pirates never mentioned the no-hitter or perfect game on the bench when the Pirates were at bat, all was quiet, except for the usual cheering for a teammate to get a hit. However each time Haddix returned to the mound, the Pirate bench yelled encouragement.

Superstition has always been a part of baseball, and it was part of Haddix's perfect game. In one of the extra innings, he stepped out of the dugout with his right foot, but suddenly returned and came out on his left foot.

Confusion at the conclusion of the game caused many of the 19, 194 fans to leave Milwaukee's County Stadium not knowing the exact score.

Felix Mantilla, who had replaced Johnny O'Brien (a former Pirate) at second base after Del Rice had filed deep as a pinch-hitter in the tenth inning, opened the thirteenth with a grounder to Don Hoak at third base. Anxious to preserve the perfect game, Hoak threw low to first base and the ball struck Rocky Nelson's left foot.

The Pirates argued that Mantilla turned to his left after reaching first base and was therefore out. They tried arguing their point with umpire Frank Dascoli, but he would not agree.

Eddie Mathews then laid down a sacrifice bunt. Haddix was ordered to intentionally walk Hank Aaron, setting up a possible double play.

Joe Adcock then hit Haddix's second pitch, a high slider, to right center. Bill Virdon leaped for the ball, but it barely dropped over the wire fence for an assumed home run.

Mantilla scored from second base, but Aaron, figuring the winning run had scored, headed across the pitcher's mound toward the Braves' dugout on the first base side. Adcock, running with his head down, continued toward third base.

The Pirates walked off the field, but the umpires and remained as Braves manager Fred Haney and the Milwaukee coaches came out to get Aaron and Adcock to touch the bases. Aaron, who hadn't touched third yet, went back to third and then second base, followed by Adcock. They ran to third base and home plate. However the umpires ruled Adcock out for passing Aaron between second and third. Only runs that would count were those scored by Mantilla and Aaron.

The following day National League President Warren Giles nullified Aaron's run and ruled that the official score of the game was 1 to 0.

In his ruling Giles stated: "While the hitter (Adcock) hit a fair ball over the field fence in flight he did not touch all bases legally and cannot be credited with a 'home run.' Since, in determining the final score, the hitter (Adcock) cannot be treated as having hit a home run but is recorded as having hit a two base hit, it is not logical to treat the base-runners as if the hitter had hit a home run."

"The score shall be determined by disregarding the 'home run' and recording it as if it would be if the batter (Adcock) had hit a two base hit, in which case only the run or runs scored which are necessary to win the game."

The Milwaukee fans were definitely on Haddix's side. They gave him a standing ovation when he struck out Lew Burdette to finish nine perfect innings and in each inning after that.

After the game a disappointed Danny Murtaugh muttered, "What a shame to lose a game for a fellow like that."

In a chair next to Haddix's locker in the Pirate clubhouse, outfielder Bill Virdon commented, "A pitcher does this once in baseball history - and we can't win the game for him."

"And to think that Adcock's ball just barely got over the fence."

Pirate pitcher Bob Friend summed it up when he said, "We're happy to be teammates of a man who pitched the greatest game in history. We were breathing with him on every pitch."

THE ALMOST PERFECT GAME

FIRST INNING
Johnny O'Brien - grounder to short
Eddie Mathews - liner to first
Hank Aaron - fly ball to center

SECOND INNING
Joe Adcock - strike out
Wes Covington - grounder to second
Del Crandall - grounder to third

THIRD INNING
Andy Pafko - fly to right
Johnny Logan - line to shortstop
Lew Burdette - strike out

FOURTH INNING
Johnny O'Brien - strike out
Eddie Mathews - fly to center
Hank Aaron - fly to center

FIFTH INNING
Joe Adcock - grounder to third
Wes Covington - fly to left
Del Crandall - fly to left

SIXTH INNING
Andy Pafko - ground out to first
Johnny Logan - ground out to shortstop

Lew Burdette - strike out

SEVENTH INNING
Johnny O'Brien - ground to third
Eddie Mathews - strike out
Hank Aaron - ground to third

EIGHTH INNNING
Joe Adcock - strike out
Wes Covington - fly to left
Del Crandall - ground to third

NINTH INNING
Andy Pafko - strike out
Johnny Logan - fly to left
Lew Burdette - strike out

TENTH INNING
Del Rice (for O'Brien) - fly to center
Eddie Mathews - fly to center
Hank Aaron - ground to shortstop

ELEVENTH INNING
Joe Adcock - ground to shortstop
Wes Covington - fly to center
Del Crandall - line to center

TWELFTH INNING
Andy Pafko - bounce back to the pitcher

Johnny Logan - fly to short left-center
Lew Burdette - ground to third

THIRTEENTH INNING
Felix Mantilla (replaced O'Brien at second) - error Hoak
Eddie Mathews - sacrifice
Hank Aaron - intentional walk
Joe Adcock - home run - later ruled a double - Mantilla scores

The other remarkable event of 1959 was ElRoy Face's 18-1 season. His winning percentage of .947, is a record that has held up, and probably will hold up for a long time to come.

Face won seventeen games in a row in relief and finished the season 18-1 with a winning percentage of .947 – a record that still stands today.

From Memorial Day, 1958 to Labor Day, 1959, ElRoy won twenty-two straight games.

Throughout his twenty-seven years as the "Voice of the Pirates," Bob Prince originated many sayings that have become a part of Pirate history. Favorites include: "You can kiss it goodby" (a home run), "By a gnat's eyelash" (a very close play or call), "Close as the fuzz on a tick's ear" (a little closer than a gnat's eyelash), A bloop and a blast (a single followed by a home run, and "A dying quail (a hit that falls in like a shot quail would..)

But the saying that became a trademark of the "come from behind" Pirates of the late '50's, and especially 1960, was: "We had 'em all the way!"

That phrase became a combination sigh of relief and an inside joke to Pirate listeners. It usually meant the somehow, some way, after being behind late in the game, the Bucs had managed to pull out a win.

ElRoy enjoyed the fruits of his "come from behind" teammates most of all in his historic 1959 season.

In that same season he also managed 10 saves, and between May 10, 1958, and September 11, 1959, he pitched in 98 games without suffering a defeat.

When the Dodgers finally defeated him 5-4, he credited his success to his teammates. "I would have lost a half-dozen times if these guys hadn't bailed me out with some runs."

ElRoy's luck didn't carry over into 1960. After losing the first game of the season, he joked, "Well, that sure takes the pressure off."

Looking at each of the games in the twenty two game streak, we can see how Face's pitching, along with his teammates "come from behind" style of play, allowed it to happen.

#1. – June 7, 1958 – Chicago

Face retired the side in the 8th in relief of Don Gross, trailing 5-3. Frank Thomas's two-run homer in the 9th tied it. Gene Freese, pinch-hitting for Face, homered to win it in the 10th.

#2. – June 21, 1958 – Los Angeles

Face relieved Ron Blackburn in the 6th with the Pirates leading 8-6. Face pitched the final four innings and won, 11-7. (Law was the Pirates' starting pitcher, relieved by Porterfield and Blackburn for one inning each. Face pitched the last four innings and was credited with the Pirates' win, at the discretion of the official scorer.

Official Baseball Rule 10.19 (c) (1) states: "When, during the Tenure of the starting pitcher, the winning team assumes the lead and maintains it to the finish of the game, credit the victory to the relief pitcher judges by the scorer to have been the mist effective."

#3. – June 29, 1958 – Chicago

With the Pirates leading after six innings, 4-3, Face relieved Bob Smith and pitched the last three innings. He was awarded the win since starter Ronnie Kilne left with the score tied, and Smith, the Reliever, pitched only 2/3 of an inning.

#4. – September 9, 1958 – San Francisco

After leading 3-2, in the Reds' eighth inning, Face relieved Law and gave up a run-scoring double (charged to Law) to tie the game. The Pirates scored in the 8th to give Face a 4-3 win.

#5 – September 9, 1958 – San Francisco

Face relieved George Witt in the top of the 9th with two out, two on, and the score tied 1-1. He got out of the inning and the Pirates won in the bottom of the 9th.

#6. – April 22, 1959 – Cincinnati

The Pirates scored seven runs in the 7th to tie the Reds, 7-1. Face relieved Bennie Daniels and gave up a home run to Gus Bell. However, the Pirates scored 2 in the bottom of the 9th to win.

#7. – April 24, 1959 – Philadelphia

Face relieved Bob Smith in the 7th leading 4-3. In the 8th he gave up 2 runs, but the Pirates scored 4 runs in the 9th to win 8-5.

#8. – May 3, 1959 – St. Louis

Face relieved Law ties 3-3 at the end of seven. In the 8th he gave up 2 runs, but the Pirates scored 4 runs in the 9th to win 8-5.

#9. – May 7, 1959 – Los Angeles

Relieving Law in the 10th tied 4-4, lead-off batter Kluszewski homered in the 10th to win the game 5-4.

#10. – May 14, 1959 – Los Angeles

Face relieved Ronnie Kline in the 7th with the Dodgers leading 4-3. He gave up three hits and two walks, but the Pirates won 5-4.

#11. – May 14, 1959 – Los Angeles

With the Pirates leading 6-3, Face relieved Friend in the 8th. He gave up 3 runs, but Dick Stuart homered in the 9th for a Pirate victory.

#12. – May 31, 1959 – Cincinnati

Face entered in the Reds' 7th. The Pirates broke an 11-11 tie in the 7th to win.

#13 – June 8, 1959 – San Francisco

Entering the 9th with a 9-9 tie, Face relieved Blackburn and the Pirates won 12-9 in the 11th.

#14 – June 11, 1959 – San Francisco

Bob Friend is relieved in the 8th with the Pirates leading 7-5. Willie Mays hit a three-run homer, but the Pirates scored 5 in the 8th to win 10-8.

#15 – June 14, 1959 – Los Angeles

Tied 3-3 in the 8th, Face relieved Alvin Jackson. The Pirates scored 3 in the 8th to win 6-3.

#16 – June 18, 1959 – Chicago

Face relieved Ronnie Kline tied 2-2 in the 9th. He and the Pirates won 4-2 in the 13th.

#17 – June 25, 1959 – San Francisco

Face came in with the score tied 1-1 in the 10th inning. He won 3-1 in the 12th.

#18 – July 9, 1959 – Chicago

With the Pirates leading 3-2 in the 9th, Face gave up the tying run, but won 4-3 in the 10th.

#19 – July 12, 1959 – St. Louis

The Pirates were leading 5-4 when Face relieved in the 8th. The Cardinals tied it in the 9th, but the Pirates won 6-5 in their half of the 10th.

#20 – August 9, 1959 – Chicago

Behind 2-1 in the 8th, Face came in and gave up another run. The Pirates tied it with another 2 runs in the 9th, and won 5-3 in the 10th.

#21 – August 23, 1959 – Los Angeles

Losing 3-2 in the 9th, Face relieved Vernon Law. The Pirates tied it in the 9th, and won in the 10th.

#22 – August 30, 1959 – Philadelphia

Face relieved Don Gross in the 10th. Eddie Bouchee broke the tie with a home run, but the Pirates came back with 2 in their half of the 10th to win 7-6.

If you look carefully at each of these games, you will see that in many there was some Pirate come from behind magic to help ElRoy and the Pirates win the game. Maybe that's why the pre-game show with General Manager Joe L. Brown used "A Little Bit of Luck" as a theme song.

Luck or not, Elroy Face managed to do something that has stood the test of time and will assure him a place in the record book for a long time to come.

CHAPTER 4
THE 1960 SEASON

The Pittsburgh Pirates' 1960 season opened April 12 against the Brave in Milwaukee's County Stadium. The Braves not only defeated the Pirates 4-3, but ElRoy Face lost in relief of starter Bob Friend. In 1959 Face had lost only once in 57 appearances.

After their brief one game road trip the Pirates returned to Pittsburgh and Forbes Field on April 14, to defeat the Cincinnati Reds 13-0 before an opening day crowd of 34,064. Vernon Law scattered seven hits to defeat the Reds for the fifth straight time, a streak that began on July 29, 1956.

On April 17, Easter Sunday, Bob Friend shut out the Reds in the first game of a doubleheader by the score of 5-0. The way the Pirates won the second game typified their come from behind spirit during the 1960 season. They rallied for six runs in the bottom of the ninth to gain a 6-5 victory. Hal Smith hit a pinch-hit three run home run and, with two outs, Bob Skinner hit a two run homer to end the game.

When Vernon Law pitched his second complete game on April 20, beating the Philadelphia Phillies, 4-2, the Pirates began a nine game winning streak, their longest since 1944. During the streak, Pittsburgh was able to move to the top of the National

League for the first time on April 24, when Harvey Haddix won 7-3 over the Milwaukee Braves. The final game in the streak was a 13-2 romp over Cincinnati for Law's fourth win in a row. The streak ended on May 2, when former Pirate Ronnie Kline, who had been traded to the Cardinals for Gino Cimoli and Tom Cheney, pitched a seven hitter to beat the Pirates 4-3. The winning run was scored when ElRoy Face issued a bases loaded walk to Carl Sawatski in the ninth inning.

The Pirates first west coast trip of the 1960 season began with the Giants in brand new Candlestick Park. Fighting for first place, the Giants swept the three game series, with Mike McCormick's 13-1 win in the finale dropping the Pirates into second place behind San Francisco.

The Dodgers continued the Pirates slump with another loss, but Law once again got them on a winning track with a 3-2 win on May 10 with the help of home runs from Hal Smith and Bill Mazeroski.

After a three game sweep of Milwaukee, which included an eight run seventh inning rally and a Clemente two run triple in the eleventh, Danny Murtaugh stated proudly, "There's always someone who doesn't believe we're licked. We've won every extra inning game we've been in."

In what eventually became a key series of the 1960 season, the Pirates swept a three game set with San Francisco, winning the final game 8-7 after coming from behind to tie the score on a dramatic two run home run by Bob Skinner in the ninth inning, and a pinch hit single off the scoreboard by Hal Smith with two out and the bases loaded in the eleventh. After Skinner's home run, his seventh of the season, Pittsburgh sportswriter, Les Biederman, wrote that "Skinner is one of the good hitters in the game because he can hit with power and also is fast enough to beat out the slow rollers. He has a good eye and can hit southpaws. His average against left-handers is above .300. He may well be the next outstanding left-handed batter in the league. Cardinal pitcher and former Pirate, Ronnie Kline, who had roomed with Skinner admitted, "Skinner is the best hitter in the league. He just can't be fooled. I curved him and he slashed a triple. Then I gave him a fast ball and he almost tore my cap off. I always thought he was a great hitter, watching him from the bench, but you know it's so when you're pitching against him."

After the three game sweep of the Giants, the level of confidence rose on the Pirates team. Third baseman Don Hoak proclaimed, "We just stomped the team we've got to beat. We can win the pennant now." And team captain Dick Groat later stated, "I think the entire squad felt confident we could take the pennant then."

The Dodgers brought everyone down a notch when they swept the Pirates in a three game series, including a Sandy Koufax one-hitter.

Realizing he needed help for Law and Friend, the only Pirates pitchers at that point with complete games, Joe Brown traded Julian Javier and Ed Bauta to the Cardinals for Wilmer "Vinegar Bend" Mizell, a left-hander who had a 1-3 record in 9 starts at that point in the season. Though his statistics coming to the Pirates were unimpressive, Mizell would prove to be a vital part of the team.

The Pirates spent the month of June in first place despite, posting a mediocre 15-11 record. Most sportswriters felt their late inning luck was running out, and were picking the Milwaukee Braves to win the National League pennant.

The Pirates responded on July 1 with a tenth inning come from behind 4-3 victory against the Dodgers. The Dodgers had taken a 3-2 lead in the tenth, but in their half of the inning, Roberto Clemente beat out an infield hit as Joe Christopher raced home from second, scoring on a head-long slide to tie the game. Dick Stuart then singled to right scoring Clemente from first with the winning run. The magic was back.

By early August the Pirates had a comfortable five and a half game lead partly due to a four game sweep of San Francisco. In typical style the Pirates literally "stole" the games. On August 6 they staged a dramatic comeback after the Giants had scored twice in the tenth inning. Their rally against pitcher Johnny Antonelli began with consecutive singles by Cimoli, Burgess and Hoak for a run. Mazeroski sacrificed, and after Stuart was passed intentionally Virdon lofted a sacrifice fly to score pinch-runner Dick Schofield with the tying run. Groat then broke up the game with a single that sent Dick Groat across the plate with the winning run. They then went on to take a double-header, taking the second game on a squeeze bunt by Dick Groat in the eighth inning that scored Mazeroski with what proved to be the winning run. When Orlando Cepada threw wild to first on Groat's bunt, Christopher raced home with an insurance run. Mazeroski had been moved to third by two consecutive bunts by Face and Christopher.

On August 14, the Pirates' lead grew to six games when they beat the St. Louis Cardinals 9-4 and 3-2. Don Hoak drove in the winning run in the second game with a single in the eleventh inning. The Pirates then proceeded to show no mercy to their cross-state rivals, the Phillies by taking both ends of a double-header on August 16. After taking the first game 11-2 behind Bob Friend, they were tied 3-3 in the second game when Buc bunts set the stage for the deciding run. Groat, Skinner and nelson all laid down successful bunt to load the bases with none out.

Robin Roberts, annoyed by the three safe bunts issued his only walk of the game, walking Roberto Clemente on four straight pitches to force in Dick Groat with the winning run.

When the Pirates dropped four straight between August 25 and 28, once again the sportswriters began predicting their collapse. Veteran Fred Lieb wrote in *The Sporting News* the "It was history repeating itself, the exact anniversary of one of the pirates' blackest weeks, the late-August, 1921 series at the Polo Grounds, in which five games were whittles off an imposing seven and one-half game lead in four days, that eventually cost the Pirates the 1921 pennant."

Gino Cimoli brushed off Lieb's comment with, "We weren't

even born when the other club was folding." The club was confident, but cautious.

On September 6, the Pirates rallied for three runs in the eighth inning to defeat the Braves, 5 to 3, but the victory proved costly for the league leaders when Dick Groat suffered a broken left wrist. In the first inning Groat noticed that third baseman Eddie Mathews was giving him the third base line. Bending further over the plate attempting to pull the ball, he saw Lew Burdette's high inside pitch heading for his head and raised his arms to protect himself. The ball hit him on the left wrist. Groat did not leave the game until the third inning when his wrist became swollen. After being X-rayed at Pittsburgh's Presbyterian Hospital, team doctor, Joseph Finegold, told Groat the wrist was broken. The players did not know the news until they read about it in the *Pittsburgh Post-Gazette* the next morning. Now even die-hard Pirate fans were wondering if their team could win the pennant without their captain, who at that time was leading both leagues with 183 hits, and was second in the National League batting race with a .325 average. Their concerns began to fade when Dick Schofield, who had spent most of his eight years with the Cardinals and Pirates on the bench, and had been hitless in his last 13 pinch-hitting appearances got 10 hits in 23 at bats for a .435 average.

On September 18, Vernon Law won his 20th game in a 5-3 victory over the Cincinnati Reds, and Mizell followed with a three-hit 1-0 shutout for his 12th win. The Pirates now needed a combination of seven wins or St. Louis defeats to clinch the pennant.

The Pirates' magic number was reduced to five on September 20, when Bob Friend broke Claude Hendrick's 48-year-old Pirate strikeout record of 176 in a 7 - 1 win over Philadelphia.

Two victories over the Cubs on September 22, 3 -2 in 11 innings, and 6 - 1, reduced the magic number to two.

Murtaugh and the pirates swept into Milwaukee on September 23 hopeful of clinching the pennant, but that afternoon St. Louis defeated the Cubs twice to prolong the issue. Before the game, Murtaugh watched Dick Groat take some swings during batting practice. Groat took a wide stance,, but stopped suddenly in the middle of his swing. When asked by his manager how it felt, Groat said that he couldn't even meet the ball; it hurt too much to go all the way through. Murtaugh encouraged him, told him it would get better and to keep working on it.

On September 25, Murtaugh allowed Don Hoak to fill out the line-up card. Cimoli replaced Virdon, whose leg was bothering him, and Hal Smith was to catch in place of Smoky Burgess. If the Cubs or pirates won, Pittsburgh would be the National League champions. That afternoon the Pirates watched the scoreboard almost as closely as Warren Spahn's pitches. Although they were defeated by the Braves 4 to 2, in 10 innings, the Pirates clinched their first pennant since 1927 when runner-up St. Louis was eliminated by a loss to the Cubs.

Murtaugh's team had a six game lead with four games left to play. The cardinals had six remaining games.

The Pittsburgh Pirates were the 1960 National League Champions.

National League Standings at the Close of the Season
October 2, 1960

	W	L	Pct.	Games Behind
Pittsburgh	95	59	.617	-
Milwaukee	88	66	.571	7
St. Louis	86	68	.558	9
Los Angeles	82	72	.513	13
San Francisco	79	75	.435	16
Cincinnati	67	87	.435	28
Chicago	60	94	.390	35
Philadelphia	59	95	.383	36

CHAPTER 5
1960 WORLD SERIES
GAME 1

The 1960 World Series began on October 5 at stately Forbes Field in Pittsburgh. Expecting a large crowd for the first Series game in Pittsburgh in thirty-five years, fans were urged by the newspapers, radio and TV not to drive to the ballpark. The biggest deterrent to driving was that parking lots were charging $5 a car. Oddsmakers were favoring the Yankees 13 to 10, but that didn't dampen the spirits of the Pirate fans.

Four former Pirate managers were present for the game: Bill McKecknie, who piloted the team in the 1925 World Series, Pie Traynor who played in the 1925 and 1927 Series, Fred Haney, skipper from 1953-1955, and Bobby Bragan, Danny Murtaugh's predecessor.

Carmen Hill, who won 22 games and pitched against the Yankees in 1927, attended compliments of his fellow employees in Indianapolis who gave him the trip as a gift. Hill started the fourth game in 1927, but was removed with the score tied 3-3. The Yankees eventually won 4-3 to take the Series.

The American League and Yankees were also well represented. Yankee owners Dan Topping and Del Webb solved the hotel problem by centering their base of operations in a private railroad car. Sitting next to the Yankee dugout were Will

Harridge, retired president of the American League, Joe Cronin, his successor, and Mrs. Cronin. Warren Giles, president of the national League was across the field next to the Pirate dugout.

The oldest fan attending was 92 year old Bertha Doak. She was the mother of Bill Doak who had pitched for the Reds, Cardinals and Dodgers from 1912-1929. She was a die-hard Pirate fan who regularly attended four out of every five games played by the Bucs at Forbes Field.

During pre-game batting practice most of the Yankees swung at the ball to see if they could drive it out of the park. Meanwhile, Mickey Mantle practiced bunting. When questioned, he responded, "I heard about the hard infield and wanted to see how far the ball would roll."

Roger Maris spent thirty minutes playing caroms off the right field wall as Coach Ralph Houk hit line drives against it. "The ball takes some bad angles when it hits the corner and you have to watch out if its right on the foul line, where that tin marker makes them bounce really funny," Maris commented. "I wish I had more time to work on it."

Before the pre-game festivities the crowd was amused by Jack Heatherington of McKeesport, a member of the Pittsburgh Skydivers Club, who parachuted from a plane circling the field. A gust of wind caught his parachute, and he landed on the roof of a warehouse across the street. Heatherington said he made the jump on a bet with a friend but denied he had attempted to land inside the park.

Before the game Bob Friend revealed that Don Hoak had played for weeks despite an 8 inch cut on his foot suffered while getting out of a swimming pool in late August. Hoak insisted that a doctor in the group of four Pirates stitch the injury even though there was no anesthetic available.

Hoak continued to play the rest of the season, often enduring extreme pain.

Finally the pre-game ceremonies began. The University of

BEAT 'EM BUCS

Pittsburgh marching band entertained and then accompanied Pittsburgh born Billy Eckstein as he sang the National Anthem.

David L. Lawrence, Governor of Pennsylvania, tossed out the first ball. He flipped it over the heads of a circle of photographers into the hands of catcher Smoky Burgess.

The Pittsburgh Pirates proved in the first game of the World Series that they were unafraid of the mighty New York Yankees, showing their opponents a little bit of everything. They executed double-plays, and made the most of their 8 hits.

Centerfielder Bill Virdon was key both on offense and defense. The Pirate first began with the Pirates behind 1 to 0 on a Roger Maris home run. Virdon worked Yankee pitcher Art Ditmar for a walk. Nervous at bat, Groat scratched his foot in the batter's box, inadvertently giving the hit-and-run sign. He stepped out, rubbed his forehead to cancel the sign, but wasn't sure Virdon had seen it. Virdon didn't. He broke for second as the pitch from Ditmar sailed past Groat. Berra caught the ball and made a perfect throw to second base, but neither Tony Kubek nor Bobby Richardson covered the base. Virdon ended up on third, and before the 23 minute inning was over, Ditmar was gone and the Pirates led 3 to 1.

In the 4th inning it was Virdon again, this time on defense. Roger Maris had opened the inning with a single and Mickey Mantle followed with a walk. Yogi Berra, in his eleventh World Series, hit the ball deep to right centerfield. Virdon and right fielder Roberto Clemente both started after the ball. Virdon got there first and grabbed the ball when they were only inches apart, stopping the 400-plus foot flight of the ball. Bill Skowron followed with an RBI single, but the rally had been stopped. After the game, Casey Stengel commented, "That stunt in center wrecked us."

Twenty-game winner Vernon Law was the winner of game one, but he ran into trouble in the eighth inning after Hector Lopez and Roger Maris, the first two Yankee batters, reached base. Murtaugh approached the mound, and after a short conference, waved his hands low and palms down - a signal that meant he wanted the little guy, ElRoy Face. Face got Mantle on a called third strike, Berra on a fly ball, and struck out Skowron on four pitches.

There were, however, some anxious moments for the Pirates and their fans in the ninth inning. After McDougald opened the inning with a single, he was forced by Richardson. But Elston Howard, pinch-hitting for Ryne Duren, the fourth Yankee pitcher, hit his fourth home run in World Series competition over the screen in right field to cut the Pirate lead in half. Then Tony Kubek, after two strikes, singled to centerfield. With two Pirates warming up in the bullpen the tying run came to the plate in Hector Lopez. Lopez grounded to Bill Mazeroski who ended the game with a routine double-play. Except for their two home runs, all the Yankee hits had been singles.

After the game, the questions began. The first was: Why had Casey Stengel started Art Ditmar instead of veteran World Series pitcher Whitey Ford? Mantle asked, "How can you not pitch your best pitcher?" Bobby Richardson also couldn't understand Casey's move. "Ford was our best pitcher," Richasrdson said, and in any big game he would be the one to start." Stengel said Forbes Field was a small park and Ditmar throws a sinker, and he wanted to save Ford for Yankee stadium. Typical Stengel double-talk. He also felt Ditmar was the Yankees' steadiest pitcher during the season. He had previously pitched 9 2/3 scoreless World Series innings.

The reporters next wanted to know why, in the second inning, Casey had pinch hit Dale long for Clete Boyer. Boyer had commented, "I was never so shocked in my life." Casey had allowed Boyer to take several steps towards the batter's box before whistling him back to the dugout.

"When Casey called me back, I thought he was going to talk to me - maybe tell me how he wanted me to swing," Boyer said. "But when he told me that Dale Long was going to hit for me, I was ready to crawl all the way home."

Casey said that he felt that since Long was a former National League player, he had a better chance with the Pirates pitchers.

Dale Long flied out and after Skinner caught Richardson's drive, Yogi Berra realized he had wandered too far off second base. Despite a head-first slide, Berra was doubled off on Skinner's throw.

Bill Mazeroski's two-run home run in Game one is often forgotten in the excitement of what was to come in Game 7. In the fourth inning, Hoak walked after there was one out.. Yankee pitcher Jim Coates had a one ball two strike count on Maz when the 24-year-old second baseman from Wheeling, West Virginia, lined a home run over the scoreboard just to the right of the left field foul line, giving the Pirates a 5 to 2 lead.

Even today Mazeroski remembers the home run. Asked how he felt after hitting it, he answers with a twinkle in hie eye. "I thought it was the greatest thing that had ever happened to me. It relaxed me for the rest of the Series."

The next batter, pitcher Vern Law was then hit on the left hand by a Coates pitch. Asked recently if he felt the pitch was in response to Mazeroski's home run, Law merely smiled.

After the game, Danny Murtaugh said it was a typical Pirate victory. They executed three double-plays, clustered their eight hits to make them more vital than the Yankees' 13, and the biggest hit of all was off the bat of Bill Mazeroski, their number 8 hitter.

This Series was not to be another mismatch between the Yankees and the Pirates as it had been in 1927.

Game 1
October 5, 1960
Forbes Field
Pittsburgh
Attendance 36,676 Time of Game - 2:29

1st Inning

YANKEES: Kubek singled off the third base bag.

Lopez hit into a double play - Mazeroski to Stuart.

Maris hit a home run into the upper deck in right field.

Mantle flied out to centerfield.

1 Run 2 Hits 0 Men Left On Base

PIRATES: Virdon walked, stole second, and went to third when Berra's throw went into centerfield because nobody covered second. Kubek was charged with an error.:

Groat doubled into the right field corner scoring Virdon.

Skinner singled to centerfield scoring Groat.

Skinner stole second.

Stuart lined to right field.

Clemente singled to centerfield scoring Skinner.

Coates came in to pitch for New York.

Burgess forced Clemente at second - Richardson to Kubek.

Hoak grounded to shortstop.

3 Runs 3 Hits 1 Man Left On Base Yankees 1 Pirates 3

2nd Inning

YANKEES: Berra singled to centerfield.

Skowron singled to right field, Berra stopped at second.

Long, pinch-hitting for Boyer, flied to right field.

Richardson lined to Skinner in left field.

Skinner threw to Mazeroski at second to double up Berra.

0 Runs 1 Hit 0 Men Left On Base

PIRATES: (McDougald replaced Boyer at third base for New York.)

Mazeroski struck out.

Law grounded to third base.

Virdon struck out.

0 Runs 0 Hits 0 Men Left On Base

Yankees 1 Pirates 3

3rd Inning

YANKEES: Coates struck out.

Kubek bounced back to the pitcher.

Lopez was thrown out by Law.

0 Runs 0 Hits 0 Men Left On Base

PIRATES: Groat singled to right-centerfield.

Skinner lined to centerfield.

Stuart singled to left field, but Groat was out going to third — Lopez to McDougald.

Stuart moved to second.

Clemente flied out to right field.

0 Runs 2 Hits 0 Men Left on Base Yankees 1 Pirates 3

4th Inning

YANKEES: Maris singled to right-centerfield.

Mantle walked.

Berra flied deep to the right-centerfield wall, but Virdon made a great catch.

Maris tagged up and went to third.

Skowron singled to left field, scoring Maris as Mantle moved to second.

McDougald fouled-out to Hoak.

Richardson flied to centerfield.

1 Run 2 Hits 1 Man Left On Base

PIRATES: Burgess flied to centerfield.

Hoak Walked.

Mazeroski hit a home run over the left field scoreboard.

Law was hit by a pitch.

Virdon fouled-out to Skowron.

Groat lined-out to Mantle in right-centerfield.

2 Runs 1 Hit 1 Man Left On Base Yankees 2 Pirates 5

5th Inning

    YANKEES: Blanchard pinch-hit for Coates and grounded to first.

Kubek singled past the pitcher's mound.

Lopez popped-up to first.

Maris fouled-out to Stuart.

0 Runs 1 Hit 1 Man Left On Base

PIRATES: (Maas came in to pitch for the Yankees.)

Skinner was safe at second when Richardson booted his ground ball into right field.

Stuart grounded to shortstop as Skinner held at second.

Clemente bounced to Kubek at shortstop who caught Skinner off second base - Richardson making the put-out.

Burgess struck out.

0 Runs 0 Hits 1 Man Left On Base Yankees 2 Pirates 5

6th Inning

YANKEES: Mantle was called out on strikes.

Berra flied to left field.

Skowron struck out.

0 Runs 0 Hits 0 Men Left On Base

PIRATES: Hoak flied to right field.

Mazeroski singled to left field.

Law sacrificed Mazeroski to second - Skowron made the unassisted put-out.

Virdon doubled off the right field screen scoring Mazeroski.

Groat grounded to shortstop.

1 Run 2 Hits 1 Man Left On Base Yankees 2 Pirates 6

7th Inning

YANKEES: McDougald grounded to shortstop.

Richardson grounded to shortstop.

Cerv pinch-hit for Maas and singled off Groat's glove.

Cerv went to second on a wild pitch.

Kubek flied out deep to left field.

0 Runs 1 Hit 1 Man Left On Base

PIRATES: (Duren came in to pitch for New York.)

Skinner was hit by a pitch.

Stuart struck out.

Clemente fouled out to Richardson in front of the first base stands.

Burgess grounded out to second base.

0 Runs 0 Hits 1 Man Left On Base Yankees 2 Pirates 6

8th Inning

YANKEES: (Cimoli replaced Skinner in left field for Pittsburgh.)

Lopez singled to right field.

Maris singled to left field as Lopez stopped at second.

(Face replaced Law for Pittsburgh.)

Mantle was called out on strikes.

Berra flied to right field.

Skowron struck out.

0 Runs 2 Hits 2 Men Left On Base

PIRATES: Mazeroski fouled out to Skowron.

Hoak singled but was out going to second - Berra to Kubek.

Face grounded out to the pitcher.

0 Runs 1 Hit 0 Men Left On Base   Yankees 2 Pirates 6

9th Inning

YANKEES: McDougald singled over Mazeroski's head.

Richardson forced McDougald at second— Mazeroski to Groat.

Howard pinch-hit for Duren and hit a home run into the lower right field seats.

Kubek singled to centerfield.

Lopez grounded into a double-play - Mazeroski to Groat to Stuart.

2 Runs 3 Hits 0 Men Left on Base

FINAL SCORE: Pirates 6 Yankees 4

CHAPTER 6
1960 WORLD SERIES
GAME 2

The sky cleared about fifteen minutes before game time after intermittent rain had fallen during the night and morning. Both clubs were deprived of infield practice when the automatic tarpaulin was rolled out due to a shower that fell at 12:25.

In order to give as many fans as possible a chance to see the Series, the Pirates sold one-game tickets as well as four-game strips. The convenience of television had made standing room tickets less attractive to fans as they were in pre-TV years. About 1,000 of 4,000 available standing room tickets available. Standing room tickets priced at four dollars were left unsold for the second game. Only about half were purchased for the opener. The press corp was another matter. The top deck press box, which had been built for the 1938 World Series at a cost of $35,000 and that was never used when the Cubs edged out the Pirates in the last days of the season, was jammed with more than 600 writers.

Before the game, Pirate manager Danny Murtaugh was forced to make some revisions to his lineup when Bob Skinner, who was hurt sliding into third base while being run down in Game 1, reported to Forbes Field with a swollen left hand and a swollen thumb. Murtaugh had planned to use right-handed hitting Dick Stuart at first base, but when Gino Cimoli, also a right-hander, went to left field for Skinner. Rocky Nelson was inserted in Stuart's place to regain some left-handed hitting in the batting order.

The second game of the Series started out as a right-handed battle between Bob Friend and Bob Turley. The Yankees began the scoring with two runs in the third inning, and one in the fourth.

Friend had struck out Skowron and Howard for the first two outs in the fourth, but then Bobby Richardson singled over second, eventually moving to third on two Burgess' passed balls. Turley helped his own cause with a single scoring Richardson.

Although Friend had struck out six in four innings and the Yankees agreed he had shown them better stuff than Vernon Law had in the opener, Murtaugh removed him in the Pirates' fourth for a pinch-hitter.

The Pirates were on the verge of knocking Turley out of the game in their half of the fourth inning. Gino Cimoli singled past a diving Skowron to open the inning. Smoky Burgess followed with another single, When Don Hoak doubled off the right field wall scoring Cimoli, the Pirates had the two tying runs in scoring position with no outs.. Casey Stengel conferred with Turley on the mound, but kept him in the game.

Bill Mazeroski then hit a low line drive that Gil McDougald grabbed. Gene Baker, hitting for Friend, popped-up to Bobby Richardson on the grass, and Bill Virdon ended the inning with a ground ball to Richardson.

Having Baker hit for Friend was a logical decision on Murtaugh's part, but it turned into a bad break for Friend.

Fred Green, Friend's replacement, walked McDougald with four successive wide pitches, but Maris forced him at second. Then, with the count two and two, Mickey Mantle stroked a line drive home run into the right centerfield seats.

But the Yankees were not finished. Elston Howard opened the sixth inning with a ball that bounced off the screen around the light tower in right centerfield eluding a leaping Virdon for a triple. Bobby Richardson then doubled to left to score Howard and finish off Green who had delivered three straight extra base hits.

Clem Labine who, as a Dodger, had defeated Turley 1 to 0 in the 1956 Series, relieved Green. Richardson took third on a passed ball, but held third while Labine threw out Turley at first. Tony Kubek then grounded to Groat, but, after looking toward Richardson at third, Groat fumbled the ball. By the time he recovered, Kubek was at first. McDougald's pinch-hit single scored Richardson, and Maris followed with a base-loading walk. Labine then struck out Mantle, but Berra drove in Kubek and McDougald with a single to centerfield.

After Skowron singled to score Maris, Murtaugh brought in George Witt to face Howard, up for the second time in the inning. Howard greeted the new pitcher with a single to center, scoring Berra, and Richardson got his second hit of the inning, a centerfield single scoring Skowron. Finally, Bob Turley flied to center to end the inning.

Joe Gibbon came in to pitch in the seventh for Pittsburgh, but fared no better than his predacessors. After singles by Kubek and DeMaestri, Mantle hit an enormous home run over the ivy-covered wall to the right of center over the 436 foot sign. Mantle became the first right-handed hitter to hit the ball over the wall in that area. It had, however been done by Dale Long, Duke Snider and Stan Musial. The ball was estimated to have traveled 478 feet.

When Mantle came to bat in the ninth against Tom Cheney, batting lefty, he received a big ovation, but was walked on four pitches.

The Pirates started some action in their half of the ninth inning when Joe Christopher was hit by a pitch Singles by Nelson and Cimoli loaded the bases with one out. Smoky Burgess then drove a smash into right field that failed to clear the screen, dropping for a single. Nelson held, unsure if Maris could catch the ball, and

Burgess was trapped at first on the return throw to Richardson. However, Richardson threw the ball wide past Skowron allowing Nelson to score and Cimoli to go to third.

Stengel then brought in Bobby Shantz who got Don Hoak to tap the ball back to the mound to start a game-ending double-play.

The 16 to 3 loss was the worst of the year for the Pirates. Their worst beating during the regular season was a 13 to 1 defeat at the hands of the Giants in San Francisco on May 8th. The 13 runners left on base by the Pirates was one short of the Series record set by the Chicago Cubs in the second game in 1910 and equaled by the Milwaukee Braves in the third game in 1957.

Danny Murtaugh took the defeat philosophically. "I prefer getting beat by a large score as long as we have to lose," he said. "We don't have to worry about a mistake that might have cost us a 2 to 1 game. I got a chance to get all my young players in. Nobody got hurt, did they? Then we're okay."

No pictures were taken in the Pirate clubhouse after their defeat. The Pirates do not request the press to stay out, but it is a Series custom that no pictures are taken in the losing clubhouse.

The Yankees, unlike the Pirates, took their time leaving for New York. They boarded a Pennsylvania Railroad sleeper which departed at 11 P.M. The Pirates left earlier in the evening on a chartered United Air Lines plane.

Game 2
October 6, 1960
Forbes Field
Pittsburgh
Attendance: 37,308 Time of Game - 3:14

1st Inning

YANKEES: Kubek singled to left field but was caught stealing second - Burgess to Mazeroski.

McDougald struck out.

Maris singled to right field.

Mantle struck out.

0 Runs 2 Hits 1 Man Left On Base

PIRATES: Virdon flied to Berra in left centerfield.

Graot grounded to second.

Clemente singled to right centerfield.

Nelson grounded to short.

0 Runs 1 Hit 1 Man Left On Base. Yankees 0 Pirates 0

2nd Inning

YANKEES: Berra grounded out - Nelson to Friend.

Skowron struck out.

Howard called out on strikes.

0 Runs 0 Hits 0 Men left On Base

PIRATES: Cimoli walked.

Burgess popped up to second.

Hoak flied to deep centerfield.
Mazeroski doubled to the left field corner.

Cimoli stopped at third.

Friend popped up to first.

0 Runs Hits 2 Men Left On Base Yankees 0 Pirates 0

3rd Inning

YANKEES: Richardson walked.

Turley sacrificed Richardson to second - friend to Mazeroski covering first.

Kubek singled to center.

Richardson scored.

McDougald doubled inside the third base line scoring Kubek.

Mantle walked.

Berra flied to centerfield.

2 Run 2 Hits 2 Men Left On Base

PIRATES: Virdon grounded out - off Turley to Kubek to Skowron.

Groat grounded to shortstop.

Clemente singled on a ball McDougald thought was going foul of third.

Nelson flied to centerfield.

0 Runs 1 Hit 1 Man Left on Base Yankees 2 Pirates 0

4th Inning

Yankees: Skowron struck out.

Howard struck out.

Richardson singled to centerfield.

Richardson went to second on a Burgess passed ball.

Turley singled to left centerfield scoring Richardson.

Kubek flied to left field.

1 Run 2 Hits 1 Man Left On Base

PIRATES: Cimoli singled to right field.

Burgess singled to right field moving Cimoli to third.

Hoak doubled off the right field wall scoring Cimoli and moving Burgess to third.

Mazeroski lined to third.

Baker pinch-hit for Friend and popped to second.

Virdon grounded to second.

1 Run 3 Hits 1 Man Left On Base Yankees 3 Pirates 1

5th Inning

YANKEES: (Green pitching for Pittsburgh.)

McDougald walked.

Maris forced McDougald at second - Nelson to Groat.

Mantle hit a home run into the lower right field seats.

Berra grounded to second.

Skowron flied to deep right field.

2 Runs 1 Hit 0 Men left On Base

PIRATES: Groat singled to centerfield.

Clemente forced Groat at second - Kubek to Richardson.

Nelson singled to left.

Clemente stopped at second..

Cimoli flied to Maris in deep right field.

Clemente moved to third after the catch.

Burgess popped up to first.

0 Runs 2 Hits 1 Man Left On Base Yankees 5 Pirates 1

6th Inning

YANKEES: Howard tripled off the left field wall.

Richardson doubled to left-center scoring Howard.

(Labine came in to pitch for Pittsburgh.)

Richardson went to third on a Burgess passed ball.

Turley grounded to the mound.

Richardson held at third base.

Kubek was safe at first on a Groat error.

Richardson held at third.

McDougald singled to left field driving in Richardson.

Kubek stopped at second.

Maris walked.

Mantle was called out on strikes.

Berra singled to left-center scoring Kubek and McDougald as Maris moved to third..

Skowron singled to left-center scoring Maris as Berra moved to third.

(Witt came in to pitch for Pittsburgh.)

Howard singled to left field scoring Berra. As Skowron stopped at second.

Richardson singled to centerfield scoring Skowron as Howard stopped at second.

Turley flied out to centerfield.

7 Runs 7 Hits 3 Men Left On Base

PIRATES: (Boyer playing third - batting fifth-, DeMaestri at short - batting second -, Kubek in left field for New York.)
Hoak doubled into the left field corner.

Mazeroski grounded back to the mound.

Hoak held at second base.

Schofield pinch-hit for Witt and singled to right field.

Hoak stopped at third base.

Virdon fouled-out to Howard.

Groat flied to right field.

0 Runs 2 Hits 2 Men Left On Base Yankees 12 Pirates 1

7th Inning

YANKEES: (Schofield at shortstop, Gibbon pitching (Batting second) for Pittsburgh.

Kubek singled to centerfield.

DeMaestri singled to right field.

Kubek stopped at second base.

Maris called out on strikes.

Mantle hit a 475 ft. home run over the centerfield wall

Boyer popped-up to second.

Skowron singled to centerfield.

Howard forced Skowron at second - Mazeroski to Schofield.

3 Runs 4 Hits 0 Men Left On Base.

PIRATES: Clemente lined to Mantle in right centerfield. Nelson grounded to second base.

Cimoli flied to right field.

0 Runs 0 Hits 0 Men Left On Base Yankees 15 Pirates 1

8th Inning

YANKEES: Richardson grounded out - Nelson to Gibbon.

Turley was called out on strikes.

Kubek flied out to left field.

0 Runs 0 Hits 0 Men Left On Base

PIRATES: Burgess walked.

Hoak flied to deep centerfield.

Mazeroski flied to left field.

Schofield walked.

Virdon grounded out to second.

0 Runs 0 Hits 2 Men Left On Base Yankees 15 Pirates 1

9th Inning

YANKEES: (Cheney pitching for Pittsburgh.)

DeMaestri called out on strikes.

Maris struck out.

Mantle walked.

Boyer doubled to left field.

Mantle moved to third.

Mantle scored and Boyer took third on a Chaney wild pitch.

Skowron grounded back to the mound.

1 Run 1 Hit 1 Man Left On Base.

PIRATES: Chrstopher, pinch-hitting foe Chaney, was hit by a pitch.

Clemente flied to left field.

Nelson singled to right field moving Christopher to second. Burgess singled high off the right field screen.

Nelson, thinking the ball might be caught, only moved to third.

Richardson's relay went wide past Skowron scoring Nelson and Cimoli going to third.

(Shantz came in to pitch for New York.)

Hoak grounded into a double play - Shantz to Richardson to Skowron.

2 Runs 2 Hits 1 Man Left On Base

FINAL SCORE: Yankees 16 Pirates 3

CHAPTER 7
1960 WORLD SERIES
GAME 3

The lop-sided Yankee victory in Game 2 raised the spirits of the Yankee fans. There were approximately 3,500 fans in line when the Stadium gates opened. Three hundred had camped at the gate all night to purchase $2.10 bleacher seats.

Dick Stuart, one of many Pirates who had never played in Yankee Stadium, was on of the first Pittsburgh players on the field for pre-game practice. He measured off the number of steps between first base and the fence in foul territory. He reported that he could take fifteen steps to his right for a foul ball.

Pirate starter "Vinegar Bend " Mizell missed the player's bus from the Hotel Commodore and had to take a taxi to yankee Stadium.

Finding that it was Danny Murtaugh's birthday, Yankee manager Casey Stengel suggested to sportswriters that they buy him a new car. Reporters joked back that they would buy the car if Casey's bank would finance it.

Pre-game ceremonies began with Lucy Monroe singing the National Anthem, accompanied by the 69th Veterans Band, as a Marine color guard raised the flag. Recently retired Boston Red Sox great Ted Williams was given the honor of throwing out the first ball to Yankee catcher Elston Howard.

In the crowd of 70,001 were former President Herbert Hoover, and Prime Minister Nehru of India, who was attending the United nations General Assembly. Nehru did not arrive until the sixth inning and missed all of the scoring.

The New York Yankees returned to Yankee Stadium to celebrate the opening home game of their 25th silver anniversary World series with another devastating victory over the Pirates.

World Series records fell as the Yankees crushed the Pirates 10 to 0. Bobby Richardson, second baseman of the Yankees, became an unlikely slugger in the rout. In 1,499 at bats in his career to that point, Richardson had hit only three home runs. His only home run in the 1960 season was on April 30, in Baltimore, against Arnold Portocarrera. But on this day he was to hit a grand slam home run and drive in six runs. He had driven in only 26 runs during the regular season. At first Richardson hadn't realized he had hit a home run. "I saw the left fielder move in while I was running to first base," he said. "Then, after I had rounded first, I saw the umpire in left field twirling his arm above his head. That's the first time I realized the ball went out of the park. I'm not sure how I felt, but I said to myself, 'How about that?' and kept on running."

Mickey Mantle also continued his assault hitting his third home run of the Series, this one off Fred Green in the fourth inning. The home run put him one away for a tie with Babe Ruth for the World Series record of fifteen.

Bob Cerv, the third different starting left fielder for the Yankees in three games, opened the first inning with a single to the left of Dick Groat. After Roger Maris drove Clemente to the wall, Mantle singled past Mizell into centerfield, moving Cerv to third. Moose Skowron then drove in Cerv with a single to centerfield.

After Gil McDougald walked on four pitches to load the bases, Murtaugh brought in Clem Labine.

Labine got two strikes on Elston Howard, but the Yankee catcher tapped an outside pitch toward third base for a single, scoring Mantle. With the bases still full, Richardson was ordered to lay down a squeeze bunt, but fouled-off the pitch. With the count 3 and 2, he homered into the lower left field seats about 30 feet from the foul line.

The rally continued with a Kubek single behind second. A Whitey Ford bunt forced him at second, but a hard block by Kubek to Dick Groat prevented a double-play. Cerv's second single of the inning caused Murtaugh to bring in Green to relieve Labine.

Maris fouled to catcher Hal Smith, and the 36 minute first inning was over.

Yankee pitcher, Whitey Ford, kept the Pirates off balance throughout most of the game. He ran through the Pirate batting order the first time without giving up a hit. In the fourth inning, he had a 3 and 1 count on Bill Virdon before the centerfielder doubled off the right field scoreboard.

Whitey Ford opened the Yankee fourth with a single. Green retired the nest two batters, but then Mantle sent his first pitch high into the upper deck in left centerfield.

Murtaugh then call on George Witt to relieve Green. McDougald beat out a slow roller to Hoak, followed by a single to right by Skowron. Elston Howard kept things going when his drive bounced off Hoak's shoe for a single, loading the bases. Richardson responded again by lining a single over short for the Yankees' final two runs. A wild pitch moved the runners to second and third, but after Kubek was walked intentionally, Ford grounded out to Mazeroski.

That was just about it until the fifth, when Maris walked with one out and was held up at third, when Mantle bounced the ball into the right field stands for a double. Skowron then grounded to Mazeroski and Maris was trapped off second. Skowron, meanwhile had rounded first as Maris was ready to dash for home. Mazeroski, after bluffing both runners, finally threw to Smith as Maris tried to score. Maris was forced to leave the game after bruising his chest on his unsuccessful slide.

Gino Cimoli received Ford's only walk in the seventh inning after a one out single by Dick Stuart, but a Hal Smith double-play ball ended the inning. Until Roberto Clemente singled in the ninth inning with two out, those were the only Pirate baserunners. After Tony Kubek bobbled a grounder by Stuart, Ford guaranteed his shutout by striking out Cimoli.

Whitey Ford had superb control while tossing the first complete World Series game since 1958. He threw 111 pitches and had a 3 ball count on a batter only three times. The Yankee left-hander said he did not become complacent with a 10 run lead. "I kept bearing down," he related. "Whenever I have a big lead like that, I just pretend the score is 2 - 1 and keep bearing down."

For the first time since 1949, Yogi Berra was not in the starting line-up of a World Series game. He did however appear in his 57th consecutive Series game when he replaced Roger Maris in the seventh. When a writer asked Casey Stengel if Yogi was unhappy, Stengel replied, "Why should he get mad? If your boss told you to take the day off, would you be mad?"

"That was a heck of a birthday present," Danny Murtaugh remarked after the game. Earlier he had received two packs of chewing tobacco from his daughter to celebrate his 43rd birthday. Asked in the locker room after the game what he would like for his birthday, Murtaugh said, "To see my 44th birthday."

Murtaugh and his wife went to see *My Fair Lady* that evening and most of the players dined with friends and relatives at "Danny's Hideaway."

The Pirates had been blown out two games in a row, but Game four would find Pirate ace Vernon Law on the mound. Law owned the lone Pirate Series win and had stopped the team's two longest losing streaks during the regular season.

It wasn't over yet.

Game 3
October 8, 1960

BEAT 'EM BUCS

Yankee Stadium
New York
Attendance 70,001 Time of Game - 2:41

1st Inning

   PIRATES: Virdon grounded to the pitcher.

   Groat grounded to second base.

   Clemente struck out.

   0 Runs 0 Hits 0 Men Left On Base

   YANKEES: Cerv singled to centerfield.

   Maris lined to Clemente in right centerfield.

   Mantle singled to centerfield.

   Cerv advanced to third.

   Skowron singled to centerfield.

   Cerv scored as Mantle moved to third.

   McDougald walked to load the bases.

   Labine came in to pitch for Pittsburgh.

   Howard beat a slow roller to third as Mantle scored.

   Richardson hit a grand slam home run just inside the foul line into the lower left field stands.

Kubek beat out a high bounce to second base.
Ford's bunt forced Kubek at second - Labine to Groat.

Cerv singled to left.

Ford stopped at second.

Green came in to pitch for Pittsburgh.

Maris foued-out to Smith.
6 Runs 6 Hits 2 Men Left on Base Pirates 0 Yankees 6

2nd Inning

PIRATES: Stuart called out on strikes.

Cimoli flied out to left field.

Smith flied out to left field.

0 Runs 0 Hits 0 Men Left On Base

YANKEES: Mantle singled to centerfield.

Mantle went to second on a wild pitch.

Skowron struck out.

Mantle was caught trying to steal third - Smith to Hoak.

McDougald struck out.

0 Runs 1 Hit 0 Men Left On Base Pirates 0 Yankees 6

3rd Inning

    PIRATES: Hoak flied to Mantle in left centerfield.

    Mazeroski grounded back to the pitcher.

    Green lined to the shortstop.

    0 Runs 0 Hits O Men Left On Base

    YANKEES: Howard flied to left field.

    Richardson struck out.

    Kubek grounded to third.

    0 Runs 0 Hits 0 Men Left On Base Pirates 0 Yankees 6

4th Inning

    PIRATES:: Virdon doubled from right centerfield.

    Groat grounded to the pitcher.

    Clemente grounded to third.

    Virdon held at second.

    Stuart flied to right field.
    0 Runs 1 Hit 1 Man Left On Base

    YANKEES: Ford singled to right centerfield.

Cerv grounded to third as Ford moved to second.

Maris grounded to second.

Ford went to third.

Mantle hit a home run into the left field bullpen.

Skowron singled to right field.

McDougald beat out hit down the third base line. Skowron moved to second.

Witt came in to pitch for Pittsburgh.

Howard beat out a single to third off Hoak.

Richardson singled to left.

Skowron and McDougald scored.

Howard went to third - Richardson second on a wild pitch.

Kubek was intentionally walked.

Ford grounded to second base.

4 Runs 6 Hits 3 Men Left On Base Pirates 0 Yankees 10

5th Inning

PIRATES: Cimoli grounded out to second.

Smith grounded to short.

Hoak flied to deep left field.

0 Runs 0 Hits 0 Men Left On Base

YANKEES: Cerv struck out.

Maris walked.

Mantle bounced a ground rule double into the right field stannd.

Maris went to third.

Skowron grounded to second, trapping Maris.

Maris was out - Mazeroski to Smith - as Mantle went to third and Skowron to second.

McDougald grounded to third base.
0 Runs 1 Hit 2 Men Left On Base Pirates 0 Yankees 10

6th Inning

PIRATES: Mazeroski singled to centerfield.

Baker pinch-hit for Witt and grounded out, Skowron to Ford.

Mazeroski went to second.

Virdon grounded to second.

Mazeroski moved to third.

Groat grounded to third.

0 Runs 1 Hit 1 Man Left On Base

YANKEES: (Chaney came in to pitch for Pittsburgh.)

Howard struck out.

Richardson flied out to center.

Kubek flied out to left field.

0 Runs 0 Hits 0 Men Left On Base Pirates 0 Yankees 10

7th Inning

PIRATES: (Berra moved to right field for New York.) Clemente flied out to right field.

Stuart singled to centerfield.

Cimoli walked.

Smith hit into a double-play - Ford to Richardson to Skowron.

0 Runs 1 Hit 1 Man Left On Base

YANKEES: Ford struck out.

Cerv flied to centerfield.

Berra singled to left centerfield.

Mantle was called out on strike
0 Runs 1 Hit 1 Man Left On Base Pirates 0 Yankees 10

8th Inning

PIRATES: Hoak grounded out to third.

Mazeroski flied out to centerfield.

Schofield pinch-hit for Chaney and lined to short.

0 Runs 0 Hits 0 Men Left On Base

YANKEES: (Gibbon came on to pitch for Pittsburgh.)

Skowron grounded out to short.

McDougald flied out to centerfield.

Howard walked.

Richardson popped-up to second.

0 Runs 0 Hits 1 Man Left On Base Pirates 0 Yankees 10

9th Inning

PIRATES: Virdon grounded out - Skowron to Ford.

Groat grounded out - Skowron to Ford.

Clemente singled to centerfield.

Stuart was safe at first on a Kubek error. Clemente moved to second.

Cimoli struck out.

0 Runs 1 Hit 2 Men Left on Base

FINAL SCORE: Pirates 0 Yankees 10

CHAPTER 8
1960 WORLD SERIES
GAME 4

Yankee fans came to Game 4 on the heels of two games that made them wonder how the Pirates had gotten into the World Series. Their home town hitters had devastated Pirate pitching, and the Pirate hitters had been blown away by Yankee pitching. Game 4 would illustrate what the "real" Pirates were all about.

Yankee pitchers and hitters weren't the only ones treating their Pittsburgh guests inhospitably. During the pre-game practice Bill Mazeroski's wife Milene came down to the railing to take a picture of her husband, but the Yankee Stadium guards wouldn't permit it.

The weekend games in New York brought a huge crowd of fans from Pittsburgh, including several busloads of steelworkers. At times the cheers for the Pirates were as noisy as the applause for the home team Yankees.

Roger Maris was back in the line-up for Game 4 after suffering a bruised chest in his home plate collision with Pirate catcher Hal Smith in the 7th inning of Game 3.

Bob Skinner, who jammed his thumb sliding into third base in the opening game, took batting practice for the first time since his injury. He had sponge rubber wrapped around the bat to absorb the shock where the injured thumb grips, but found it still too painful to play. "I caught a line-drive during practice and I thought my whole thumb was going to come off, " Skinner confessed. The suggestion to use Novocain to deaden the pain was rejected.

To many, Game 4 was, arguably, the finest game of the 1960 World Series. The Pirates had a four-run lead going into the ninth inning of their 6-4 victory in the first game, but in Game 4 they trailed 1-0, went into the lead with three runs in the fifth inning off Ralph Terry, and used exceptional pitching and fielding to grab the win.

Their 3-2 victory assured that for the sixth consecutive year it would take at least six games to declare the champions. It also meant the Series would go back to Pittsburgh for the conclusion.

Under the Stadium lights, which had been turned on to provide more light for the color TV cameras, the Pirates made one of the most dramatic comebacks in World Series history. They got three runs in the fifth when they broke through against Ralph Terry. Starter Vernon Law supplied the key hit, a double after two outs. After Law was relieved in the seventh, ElRoy Face set down the eight Yankees that faced him with his amazing fork ball and help in the field from Bill Virdon and Don Hioak.

Prior to the outburst in the fifth inning, Ralph Terry had experienced a rather easy outing. In the first three innings the only base runner was Smoky Burgess who had walked. Terry had an easy fourth, and was helped when Bill Skowron slammed a home run in the New York half of the inning. But all this ended when the Pirates came to bat in the fifth. After thirteen successive scoreless innings the Pirate magic returned.

Gino Cimoli opened with a single that dropped in front of Roger Maris. Then Skowron went to his right for a half-speed roller by Burgess. Trying for a force play at second, the ball was late and the Pirates had two men on.

Don Hoak then tried to push a bunt over the heads of Richardson and Skowron, but Richardson caught his pop-fly. When Skowron caught Bill Mazeroski's pop-fly near the mound, it seemed as if terry had pitched out of the jam. But Vernon Law, a .181 hitter during the season, lined Terry's first pitch to left. The ball bounced against the low barrier and Cimoli scored the tying run as Law went to second. Terry then had 2 strikes on Bill Virdon when "the quail" dropped a single in front of the charging Mantle, scoring Burgess and Law. Captain Dick Groat popped up to end the inning but the Pirates led 3-1.

The Pirates threatened again in the seventh inning. After Hoak lined the first pitch to centerfield for a single, Mazeroski successfully laid down a sacrifice bunt. Law then continued his hitting streak with a liner that bounced off McDougald's glove into foul territory for a single that moved Hoak to third.

Stengel had seen enough and called in southpaw Bobby Shantz. After striking out Virdon, he got Groat to ground into a force-out, ending the threat.

In the Yankee seventh, Skowron led off with a shot off the white foul pole for a ground-rule double. McDougald then dropped a single in front of Clemente in right field, sending Skowron to third.

Murtaugh went to the mound to confer with Law and decided to leave him in.

Skowron then scored when Richardson grounded to Mazeroski for a force-out, but his throw to first was late.

When John Blanchard, pinch-hitting for Shantz, drilled a single into right field, Murtaugh decided it was time for Face.

Bob Cerv hit a tremendous drive to right-centerfield, but Virdon caught up with the ball at the 407 foot marker. Face then finished off the inning by fielding a bouncing ball hit by Kubek.

Both Face and Shantz' replacement, Jim Coates, pitched a non-eventful eighth inning.

In the ninth, Mickey Mantle demonstrated that he could play center as well as Virdon when he made a running one-handed catch in deep right centerfield on a ball hit by Don Hoak.

Taking the field in the ninth, Bob Oldis came in to catch for Pittsburgh for defensive insurance. Skowron promptly hammered a long drive to right, but it curved foul. Then, on a 2 and 2 count, Skowron lined the ball down the third base line. Hoak shifted his glove to the right, made the stop, and threw to Stuart for the out. McDougald followed with a liner to Groat, and Long ended the game with a fly ball to Clemente.

After the game Mickey Mantle and Yogi Berra had nothing but praise for Roy Face. "They talk about his forkball and you get the wrong idea," Mantle said. "He's no junk pitcher. He's quick. His fast ball is plenty fast enough." Yogi commented, "He has a funny, little jiggling motion as he lets go of the ball that confuses you a little. I suppose after a while you get used to it."

Roy Face did not see the pirates score their 3 runs in the fifth inning. Bull pen catcher Bob Oldis commented, "We're not exactly superstitious. But we like to change things around when we aren't winning, like our seats. That's how come Face didn't see the inning. He had decided to sit with his back to the field."

Mantle credited Bill Virdon with keeping the Pirates in the Series. "He's made two great catches that saved victories for them in the first and fourth games," said Mantle. "If it hadn't been for him, we probably would have the Series all wrapped up by now and been on our way home."

Bill's response was, "I guess it's better to be lucky than good. I've been lucky in the outfield and today I was lucky at the plate. Ralph Terry had two strikes on me and hung a curve up high and I hit it for a two-run single."

After the game the Yankees complained that they had been hurt by the umpires on two decisions. Yogi Berra felt that he had beaten Don Hoak's throw to first for the double-play that took Vernon Law out of a first inning jam, and Bill Stafford thought his throw to second base for an attempted force-out in the 5th inning beat Gino Cimoli to the bag.

Manager Casey Stengel would not support criticism of Bill Skowron because of his late throw to second that set up Pittsburgh's three-run inning. "If the play was as close as it looked, he had to try to get the man," said Casey. "Besides, we had our chances to score and there were some mistakes made by the pitchers that didn't help us."

The Yankees had 56 hits, 32 runs and 7 home runs. The Pirates 32 hits, 12 runs and 1 home run. But the Series was even at 2-2.

Game 4
October 9, 1960
Yankee Stadium
New York
Attendance 67,812 Time of Game - 2:29

1st Inning

PIRATES: Virdon struck out.

Groat popped out to second.

Clemente struck out.

0 Runs 0 Hits 0 Men Left On Base

YANKEES: Cerv singled to centerfield. Kubek doubled to left field.

Cerv moved to third.

Maris flied out to short right.

Mantle was walked intentionally.

Berra hit into a double play - Hoak forcing Kubek to Stuart.

0 Runs 2 Hits 1 Man Left On Base Pirates 0 Yankees 0

2nd Inning

    PIRATES: Stuart popped out to third.

    Cimoli rapped to the mound.

    Burgess walked.

    Hoak lined to left field.

    0 Runs 0 Hits 0 Men Left On Base

    YANKEES: Skowron tapped back to the pitcher.

    McDougald lined out to right field.

    Richardson doubled down the left field line.

    Terry grounded out - Law to Stuart.

    0 Runs 1 Hit 1 Man Left On Base Pirates 0 Yankees 0

3rd Inning

    PIRATES: Mazeroski struck out.

    Law was called out on strikes.

    Virdon grounded out to second base.

    0 Runs 0 Hits 0 Men Left On Base

YANKEES: Cerv grounded to shortstop.

Kubek popped-up to Mazeroski behind first base.

Maris grounded out to second.

0 Runs 0 Hits 0 Men Left On Base Pirates 0 Yankees 0

4th Inning

PIRATES: Groat flied to centerfield.

Clemente struck out.

Stuart grounded off Terry to Kubek who threw him out at first.

0 Runs 0 Hits 0 Men Left On Base

YANKEES: Mantle struck out after bunting foul on the third strike.

Berra grounded back to the pitcher.

Skowron hit a home run into the lower right field seats.

McDougald struck out.

1 Run 1 Hit 0 Men Left On Base Pirates 0 Yankees 1

5th Inning

PIRATES: Cimoli singled to right field.

Burgess was safe on a fielder's choice when Skowron threw late to second attempting a force out.

Hoak popped-up to Richardson on a bunt attempt.

Mazeroski popped up to first.

Law doubled off the fence in the left field corner.

Cimoli scored and Burgess went to third.

Virdon singled to centerfield scoring Burgess and Law.

Virdon went to third on Mantle's throw to the plate.

Groat popped-up to second.

3 Runs 3 Hits 1 Man Left On Base

YANKEES: Richardson singled over Stuart's head.

Terry struck out.

Cerv struck out.

Kubek struck out.

0 Runs 1 Hit 1 Man Left On Base Pirates 3 Yankees 1

6th Inning

PIRATES: Clemente singled to right field.

Stuart rolled to third.

Clemente moved to second.

Cimoli grounded to second.

Clemente went to third.

Burgess flied out to deep right field.

0 Runs 1 Hit 1 Man Left On Base

YANKEES: Maris grounded to second base.

Mantle flied out to right field.

Berra grounded out to second.

0 Runs 0 Hits 0 Men Left On Base Pirates 3 Yankees 1

7th Inning:

PIRATES: Hoak singled to centerfield.

Mazeroski sacrificed Hoak to second - Terry to Richardson.

Law singled.

Hoak moved to third.

(Shantz came in to pitch for new York.)

Virdon struck out.

Groat forced Law at second - Kubek to Richardson.

0 Runs 2 Hits 1 Man Left On Base

YANKEES: Skowron bounced a ground-rule double into the right field stands.

McDougald singled to right field.

Skowron moved to third.

Richardson forced McDougald at second - Mazeroski unassisted.

Skowron scored.

Blanchard pinch-hit for Shantz and singled past first base.

Richardson moved to second.

(Face came in to pitch for Pittsburgh.)

DeMaestri ran for Blanchard.

Cerv flied out deep to right center where Virdon made a leaping catch.

Richardson moved to third.

Kubek grounded back to the mound.

1 Run 3 Hits 2 Men Left On Base Pirates 3 Yankees 2

8th Inning

PIRATES: (Coates came in to pitch for New York.)

Clemente tapped to second base.

Stuart popped-up to second.

Cimoli rolled back to the mound.

0 Runs 0 Hits 0 Men Left On Base

YANKEES: Maris flied to centerfield.

Mantle struck out - Burgess dropped the ball and had to throw him out.

Berra grounded out to third.

0 Runs 0 Hits 0 Men Left On Base Pirates 3 Yankees 2

9th Inning

PIRATES: Burgess grounded out - Skowron to Coates

Hoak flied out to right centerfield.

Mazeroski singled to right field.

Face struck out.

0 Runs 1 Hit 1 Man Left On Base

YANKEES: (Oldis came in to catch for Pittsburgh.)

Skowron grounded to Hoak.

McDougald lined-out to shortstop.

Long pinch-hit for Richardson and flied to right field.

0 Runs 0 Hits 0 Men Left On Base

FINAL SCORE: Pirates 3 Yankees 2

Game 1: Starting Pitchers Art Ditmar and Vernon Law

Game 2: Starting Pitchers Bob Turley and Bob Friend

Game 3: Starting Pitchers Vinegar Bend Mizell and Whitey Ford

Game 4: Starting Pitchers Vernon Law and Ralph Terry

Game 5: Starting Pitchers Harvey Haddix and Art Ditmar

Game 6: Starting Pitchers Whitey Ford and Bob Friend

Game 7: Starting Pitchers Bob Turley and Vernon Law

Pirates celebrate winning the National League pennant

ElRoy Face relieves Vernon Law in Game 1

Mazeroski cuts down Tony Kubek in Game 1

Danny Murtaugh views the action from the dugout

George Witt, ElRoy Face, Joe Gibbon and Dick Groat view the Babe Ruth Monument at Yankee Stadium

ElRoy Face racked up three saves in the Series

Tony Kubek after getting hit in the throat in the eighth inning of Game 7

Gino Cimoli celebrates in the Victorious Pirate clubhouse after Game 7

CHAPTER 9
1960 WORLD SERIES
GAME 5

Many of the sportswriters questioned Yankee manager Casey Stengel about starting Art Ditmar. His response was: "Well, I'll tell you. I spoke to the Baltimore writers and they've got the best pitching staff in the league and so I figure they know more about it than anybody else. They advised that I go with Ditmar." In typical Stengel style he concluded his remark with a wink.

Later Casey turned to John Carmichael, long time friend and sports editor of the Chicago Daily News, and asked him who he thought would be managing the Cubs in the coming season. "I don't know," Carmichael replied. "But the way you're going, they may even make you an offer."

When asked by reporters what the Pirates were paying him, ElRoy Face replied, "That's between me and Joe Brown." Remembering he had left someone out, he quickly added, "And my wife."

ElRoy Face's spectacular Series performance may have been motivated by more than the money involved. Before the game he sent a program over to the Yankee clubhouse to be autographed. It came back without a single signature.

In the Yankee first inning, with two out, Bob Cerv beat out a slow roller to Don Hoak, then went to second on Hoak's wild throw. Haddix then walked Mantle intentionally, but struck out Skowron to retire the side.

The Pirates' big inning was the second, which Dick Stuart started with a line single to left field. Gino Cimoli hit a slow bouncing ball to Bobby Richardson near second base. He tagged Stuart, but had no chance for a double-play. Smoky Burgess lined a double down the right field line on the first pitch from Ditmar.

Don Hoak topped the ball to Kubek who couldn't get to the ball quickly enough to keep Cimoli from scoring. Meanwhile, Burgess had committed and was running to third as Kubek threw to McDougald. Burgess stopped at third when the ball got away from McDougald, and Hoak went to second.

After taking a ball, Mazeroski hit a high chopper. The ball took an extremely high bounce and rolled into left field for a double. Burgess and Hoak both scored.

Luis Arroyo, a former Pirate, then entered the game for New York, promptly striking out Haddix and getting Virdon to foul-out to McDougald. At rhe end of two innings the Pirates led 2-0.

Catcher Elson Howard opened the Yankee half of the second with a hit that went to the right field wall for a double. When Richardson ground-out, Mazeroski to Haddix, Howard took third and then scored when Kubek grounded to Stuart. Arroyo then grounded to Groat for the third out.

The Pirates quickly disposed of Arroyo in the third. Groat doubled off the left field fence, followed by a single to left by Clemente that scored the team captain.

Stengel decided that was enough, and brought in Bill Stafford, who promptly retired the next three batters.

In the Yankee at bat, with a 3-0 count, McDougald bounced to Haddix. Roger Maris then hit a 3 and 1 pitch into the third tier of the right field stands for a home run, cutting the Pirate lead in half.

The Pirate fourth had some strange plays, but the Yankees worked out of it. Leading off, Hoak got a hit on a ball that took a bounce right as Kubek was ready to field it. Then, after Mazeroski grounded to Kubek for the beginning of what seemed to be a double-play, Richardson threw past first putting Maz on base. Stafford got Haddix to hit into a double-play that ended the inning without any runs being scored.

The Pirates were guilty of two errant plays in the Yankee fourth, but New York failed to capitalize. It began when Howard was safe at first on a high throw from Groat. The error cancelled out, however, when Mazeroski caught Richardson's liner and doubled Howard off first. Kubek struck out for what should have been the third out, but ended up on base when Burgess was charged with his third passed ball, a World Series record. Fortunately, Haddix struck out Stafford for the final out.

Both Haddix and Stafford were in command through the sixth inning, but with two out in the Pirate seventh, Haddix beat out a hit in back of first, followed by a Bill Virdon double off of first baseman Bill Skowron's glove. With men on second and third, Groat flied to Cerv in left field to end the threat.

Don Hoak made what Danny Murtaugh said afterwards was the most vital defensive play of the game, when he grabbed a low-liner off the bat of Bobby Richardson. What followed could have been disastrous for the Prates if not for that play.

Kubek hit Hddix's first pitch for a single to center. Hector Lopez, hitting for Stafford, hit another first pitch to right for a single.

Murtaugh felt it was time for ElRoy. Face got McDougald to force Kubek, Mazeroski to Groat, bringing up Maris. After two fouls, Face got him with a fork-ball, ending the inning with no runs scored.

Ryne Duren, Staffords replacement, got through the Pirate eighth without any problems. Meanwhile, Face was looking at the Yankee power hitters. Bob Cerv flied-out to Virdon in in right-center, and, for the seventh time in the Series, Mantle walked - on four pitches. Moose Skowron excited the crowd with a foul home run to left, but eventually popped-up to Groat near the third base foul line. Berra, batting for Howard and appearing in his sixty-sixth Series game, grounded to Mazeroski.

After the Yankee Stadium lights were turned on, the Pirates added an insurance run to their total when Burgess singled to left to open the ninth inning, going to second when Cerv bobbled the ball.

Joe Christopher, running for Burgess, went to third on a Duren wild pitch off of Berra's glove. Christopher scored when Duren just missed a ball hit by Hoak. Duren got by Mazeroski, Face and Virdon with no further scoring.

With Bob Oldis, the Pirates' best defensive catcher as his battery mate, Face finished off the ninth. Dick Groat threw out Richardson, and then fielded Kubek's high pop-up near first base for out number two.

John Blanchard, hitting for Duren, sent Clemente to the warning track, but the game was over.

Face and the Pirates had done it again. They were up three games to two and heading back to Pittsburgh.

Questioned again after the game concerning his choice of Art Ditmar, Stengel this time responded, "After all, the fella is experienced and he was my top winner with 15 victories. He certainly had plenty of rest, too, didn't he?"

Another reporter asked Casey if he would call the Yankee position "desperate." Casey replied, "You can call it that, if you like. I won't. But I can count, you know!"

The Yankee manager also complained that the lights were turned on too late in the game. "Both sides quit hittin' in the seventh and eighth and, when they got the lights on in the ninth, it was too late."

Meanwhile, a stewardess on the Pirates' chartered plane, in an attempt to be hospitable, offered a toast to the Pirates as the plane landed at the Pittsburgh airport. Obviously not a baseball fan she declared: "Here's to then next world's champions, the Pittsburgh Steelers!"

Game 5
October 10, 1960
Yankee Stadium
New York
Attendance 62,753 Time of Game - 2:32

1st Inning

    PIRATES: Virdon fouled-out to Howard.

    Groat flied to left.

    Clemente grounded to shortstop.

    0 Runs 0 Hits 0 Men Left On Base

    YANKEES: McDougald bunted out to third base.

    Maris grounded out to second.

    Cerv singled on a slow roller to third.

    Hoak's throwing error moved Cerv to second.

    Mantle was walked intentionally.

    Skowron struck out.

    0 Runs 1 Hit 2 Men Left On Base Pirates 0 Yankees 0

2nd Inning

PIRATES: Stuart singled to left field.

Cimoli forced Stuart unassisted to Richardson.

Burgess doubled into the right field corner.

Cimoli moved to third.

Hoak bounced to Kubek.

Kubek threw to McDougald trying to get Burgess at third. McDougald dropped the ball for an error.

Cimoli scored.

Hoak moved to second.

Mazeroski doubled down the left field line.

Burgess and Hoak scored.

Arroyo came in to pitch for New York.

Haddix struck out.

Virdon fouled to McDougald.

3 Runs 3 Hits 1 Man Left On Base

YANKEES: Howard doubled off the right field wall.

Richardson grounded out - Mazeroski to Haddix covering first.

Howard went to third.

Kubek grounded to first.

Howard scored.

Arroyo grounded to short.

1 Run 1 Hit 0 Men Left On Base Pirates 3 Yankees 1

3rd Inning

PIRATES: Groat doubled into the left field corner.

Clemente singled to left field.

Groat scored.

Stafford came in to pitch for New York.

Stuart popped up to third.

Cimoli flied out to right field.

Burgess grounded out to second.

1 Run 2 Hits 1 Man Left On Base

YANKEES: McDougald grounded back to the mound.

Maris hit a home run into the third deck of the right field stands.

Cerv grounded out to second.

Mantle walked.
Skowron flied out to right field.

1 Run 1 Hit 1 Man Left On Base Pirates 4 Yankees 2

4th Inning

PIRATES: Hoak singled off Kubek's chest.

Mazeroski forced Hoak at second - McDougald to Richardson.

Haddix hit into a double play - Stafford to Kubek to Skowron.

0 Runs 1 Hit 0 Men Left On Base

YANKEES: Howard was safe at first on an error by Groat. His throw pulled Stuart off the bag.

Richardson lined into a double play - Mazeroski to Stuart.

Kubek struck out but went to first on a Burgess passed ball.

Stafford struck out.
0 Runs 0 Hits 1 Man Left On Base. Pirates 4 Yankees 2

5th Inning

PIRATES: Virdon grounded out to third.

Groat grounded out to short.

Clemente grounded to short.

0 Runs 0 Hits 0 Men Left On Base

YANKEES: McDougald flied to right field.

Maris popped-up to short.

Cerv struck out.

0 Runs 0 Hits 0 Men Left On Base Pirates 4 Yankees 2

6th Inning

PIRATES: Stuart round out to third base.

Cimoli struck out.

Burgess flied to centerfield.

0 Runs 0 Hits 0 Men Left On Base

YANKEES: Mantle struck out.

Skowron grounded to shortstop.

Howard was called out on strikes.

0 Runs 0 Hits 0 Men Left On Base Pirates 4 Yankees 2

7th Inning

PIRATES: Hoak struck out.
Mazeroski flied out to short left field.

Haddix beat out a hit behind second base.

Virdon doubled off Skowron's glove down the right field line.

Haddix moved to third.

Groat flied out to left field.

0 Runs 2 Hits 2 Men Left On Base

YANKEES: Richardson lined out to third.

Kubek singled to centerfield.

Lopez pinch-hit for Stafford and singled to right field.

Kubek stopped at second base. 8th

(Face came in to pitch for Pittsburgh.)

McDougald forced Lopez at second base - Groat to Mazeroski

- but missed the double play.

    Kubek moved to third base.

    Maris struck out.

    0 Runs 2 Hits 2 Men Left On Base Pirates 4 Yankees 2

8th Inning

    PIRATES: (Duren came in to pitch for New York.)

    Clemente struck out.

    Stuart flied to left field.

    Cimoli was called out on strikes.

    0 Runs 0 Hits 0 Men Left on Base

    YANKEES: (Nelson came in to play first for Pittsburgh.)

    Cerv flied out to deep centerfield

    Mantle walked.

    Skowron popped-up to short.

    Berra pinch-hit for Howard and grounded out to second.

    0 Runs 0 Hits 1 Man Left On Base Pirates 4 Yankees 2

9th Inning

PIRATES: (Berra came in to catch for New york.)

Burgess singled to left field and went to second on Cerv's error.

Christopher ran for Burgess.

Christopher went to third on a wild pitch.

Hoak singled through the box scoring Christopher.

Mazeroski struck out.

Face struck out bunting the third strike foul.

Virdon grounded back to the pitcher.

1 Run 2 Hits 1 Man Left On Base

YANKEES: (Oldis came in to pitch for Pittsburgh.)

Richardson grounded out to shortstop.

Kubek popped up to short.

Blanchard pinch-hit for Duren and flied to deep right field.

0 Runs 0 Hits 0 Men Left On Base

FINAL SCORE: Pirates 5 Yankees 2

CHAPTER 10
1960 WORLD SERIES
GAME 6

As the Series returned to Pittsburgh and Forbes Field for Game 6, the Pirates' regular fans, the ordinary people who form the bulk of their supporters, predominated the crowd. The fans began arriving early with lines for standing- room tickets stretching through Schenley Park across Panther Hollow Bridge and around the rear of Phipps Conservatory. The crowd eventually totaled 38,580. Benny Benack and his Iron City Six serenaded the fans with, "The Bucs Are Goin' All The Way', the Pirate fight song, at the main entrance an hour before game time.

At his daily meeting with the writers in the Yankee dugout, Casey Stengel explained why Whitey Ford was his choice for starting pitcher: "If I'd have taken a vote of my fellers, you now what could have happened? Ford would have gotten all the votes but maybe six or eight and the reason he wouldn't have gotten those six or eight is because some of the pitchers would have voted for themselves."

Pitcher Whitey Ford didn't know until 11 o'clock that he would be the Yankees' starting pitcher. "I had an idea I was going," he said, "but I wasn't sure."

Continuing in the double-talk that has made him famous, Casey continued, "Turley does better as a relief pitcher than Ford. I tried Ford in relief in a game up in Boston. The Red Sox had the bases full. Vic Wertz was coming to bat so I took out Turley and put in Ford. I figured Wertz would never hit one in the bleachers off'n Whitey. But Wertz did. So I knew that Ford doesn't do so well in relief as he does in starting. And I know that Turley pitched good in relief for me in the World Series against Milwaukee. That is how I picked Ford to be my starter for the sixth game."

Game 6
October 12, 1960
Forbes Field
Pittsburgh
Attendance 38,580 Time of Game: 2:38

1st Inning

YANKEES: Boyer grounded back to the pitcher.

Kubek grounded to second.

Maris flied to centerfield.

0 Runs 0 Hits 0 Men Left On Base

PIRATES: Virdon singled to centerfield.

Groat grounded into a double-play - Richardson to Kubek to Skowron.

Clemente singled to right field.

Stuart struck out.

BEAT 'EM BUCS

0 Runs 2 Hits 1 Man Left On Base Yankees 0 Pirates 0

2nd Inning

YANKEES: Mantle grounded back to the pitcher.

Berra walked.

Skowron singled to right field.

Berra moved to third.

Howard was hit by a pitched ball.

Grba ran for Howard.

Richardson flied to short centerfield.

Ford singled back to Friend.

Berra just beat out the throw to score.

Boyer struck out.

1 Run 2 Hits 3 Men Left On Base

PIRATES: (Blanchard went in to catch for new York.)

Cimoli grounded to third.

Smith singled to left field.

Hoak forced Smith at second - McDougald to Richardson.

Mazeroski lined to centerfield.

0 Runs 1 Hit 1 Man Left On Base Yankees 1 Pirates 0

3rd Inning

YANKEES: Kubek was hit by a pitched ball.

Maris doubled off the right field screen.

Kubek went to third.

Mantle singled to right field.

Kubek and Maris scored.

Berra singled to right centerfield.

Mantle moved to third.
(Cheney came in to pitch for Pittsburgh.)

Skowron hit a sacrifice fly to deep right-center.

Mantle scored.

Blanchard singled to centerfield.

Berra stopped at second.

Richardson tripled off the left field scoreboard.

Berra and Blanchard scored.

Ford was called out on strikes.

Boyer flied to centerfield.
5 Runs 5 Hits 1 Man Left on Base

PIRATES: Baker batted for Cheney and struck out.

Virdon grounded to second.
Groat struck out.

0 Runs 0 Hits 0 Men Left On Base Yankees 6 Pirates 0

4th Inning

YANKEES: (Mizell came in to pitch for Pittsburgh.)

Kubek flied out to right field.

Maris struck out.

Mantle walked.

Berra grounded to first.

0 Runs 0 Hits 1 Man Left On Base

PIRATES: Clemente rounded to short.

Stuart grounded to short.

Cimoli was called out on strikes.

0 Runs 0 Hits 0 Men Left On Base Yankees 6 Pirates 0

5th Inning:

YANKEES: Skowron doubled off the left-centerfield wall.

Blanchard flied to deep right.

Skowron went to third.

Richardson lined to third.

Ford grounded to second.

0 Runs 1 Hit 1 Man Left On Base

PIRATES: Smith singled to centerfield.

Hoak walked.

Mazeroski grounded into a double-play - Boyer to Richardson to Skowron.

Smith moved to third.

Nelson pinch-hit for Mizell and struck out.

0 Runs 1 Hit 1 Man Left On Base Yankees 6 Pirates 0

6th Inning

YANKEES: (Green came in to pitch for Pittsburgh.)

Boyer tripled off the right centerfield wall.

Kubek singled to right field.

Boyer scored.

Maris singled to right field.

Kubek moved to third.

(Labine came in to pitch for Pittsburgh.)

Mantle struck out.

Berra singled to right field.

Kubek scored.

Maris went to third.

Skowron hit into a double-play - Groat to Mazeroski to Stuart.

2 Runs 4 Hits 1 Man Left On Base

PIRATES: Virdon grounded out to second.

Groat flied out to right field.

Clemente singled to centerfield.

Stuart bounced back to the pitcher.

0 Runs 1 Hit ! Man Left On Base Yankees 8 Pirates 0

7th Inning

YANKEES: Blanchard doubled off the right field screen.

Richardson tripled off the left-centerfield wall scoring Blanchard.

Ford bunted.

Richardson scored ahead of Hoak's throw.

Boyer hit into a double play - Hoak to Mazeroski to Stuart.

Kubek flied to centerfield.

2 Runs 3 Hits 0 Men Left On Base

PIRATES: Cimoli was safe on Kubek's error.

Smith forced Cimoli at second - Kubek to Richardson.

Hoak forced Smith on a bunt - Blanchard to Kubek,

Mazeroski flied to centerfield.

0 Runs 0 Hits 1 Man Left On Base Yankeed 10 Pirates 0

8th Inning

YANKEES: Maris singled to right field.

Mantle forced Maris at second - Mazeroski to Groat.

Mantle went to second on a wild pitch.

Berra singled to centerfield scoring Mantle.

Berra took second on Virdon's throwing error to home.

Skowron grounded to second moving Berra to third.

Blanchard doubled off the right field screen scoring Berra.

Richardson flied out to left field.

2 Runs 3 Hits 1 Man Left On Base

PIRATES: (Kubek moved to left field and DeMaestri to shortstop for New York.)

Schofield pinch-hit for Labine and grounded to third.

Virdon grounded to second.

Groat singled off DeMaestri's glove.

Clemente grounded out to short.

0 Runs 1 Hit 1 Man Left On Base Yankees 12 Pirates 0

9th Inning

YANKEES: (Witt came in to pitch for Pittsburgh - Schofield to shortstop.)

Ford grounded out to first.

Boyer grounded to second.

Kubek lined to right.

0 Runs 0 Hits 0 Men Left On Base

PIRATES: Stuart grounded to shortstop.

Cimoli singled to right field.

Smith hit into a double-play - Boyer to Richardson to Skowron

0 Runs 1 Hit 0 Men Left On Base

FINAL SCORE: Yankees 12 Pirates 0

CHAPTER 11
1960 WORLD SERIES
GAME 7

Even though they had been pounded three times, the Pirates were still there for the final game that would decide the world championship. Don Hoak felt that the 12-0 romp in Game 6 became a motivation. "The sixth game loss was the turning point for the team emotionally," Hoak insisted. "We had a short team meeting and everybody agreed we already had a great year. We could get beat fifteen to nothing tomorrow, but still would have had a great season. We were more relaxed for the seventh game than any game in the Series."

Manager Danny Murtaugh embellished a Bible quote prior to the start of the game when he stated to reporters, "Everybody else but Law will be in the bull pen, and if I may give you a twisted quote from the Bible, many are chosen, but I hope few will be called."

A conservative crowd entered Forbes Field for Game 7. Watching fans collect outside the ball park, police Inspector Vincent Dixon commented, "Everybody's in a daze. They're confused. They took a beating and they know it."

Hoping to arouse some pre-game excitement, Benny Bennack and his band once again played every song they could think of at the corner of Sennott and Bouquet Street. But other than for an occasional cheer of "Beat 'em Bucs," the crowd was unresponsive. Marcy Lynn, the band's vocalist, was somewhat prophetic when she commented, "These people are so quiet. I think they are afraid to get excited. But we'll be here after the game and they'll be excited then."

Leo Parker, a concessionaire, held the same optimism. "The spirit of the crowd is gone," he said, "But after the game - watch out. They'll go crazy."

The Pittsburgh parking lot ordinance, enacted to protect World Series fans from sudden price increases, failed in its aim. In most of the lots, prices, which had been dropped to $2, were back up to $5. Even so, most lots were full or nearly full.

Lieutenant Carl Basil of the traffic division believed that many drove into Oakland after reading that the fees were down. Once there, they had no choice but to park and pay the going rate.

A very legal-looking document appeared on the door of the office of Thomas E. Barrett, Allegheny County Clerk of Courts in the County Courthouse on the morning of Game 7.

An official order, signed by Judge Samuel A. Weiss, authorized the Clerk of Courts to close at 12:30 p.m. Underneath the order was a supplementary document, not signed by Judge Weiss, stating: "Our other grandmother died. - We have gone to bury her with the Yanks."

For five innings it looked as if the Pirates' Vernon Law was headed for a record-tying third Series win, Two new faces in the line-up, Bob Skinner and Rocky Nelson, combined for a 2-0 lead off Yankee pitcher Bob Turley in the first inning. Skinner walked and Rocky Nelson slammed a two-run homer over the screen in right field.

In the second inning, it quickly became 4 to 0. Smoky Burgess rammed a pitch inside the first base line into the right field corner. Roger Maris' quick recovery held it to a single. Bill Stafford replaced Turley and walked Don Hoak on four straight pitches. Bill Mazeroski then bunted down the third base line and beat Stafford's off-balance throw to fill the bases. Pirate pitcher

Vernon Law then hit a one-bouncer to Stafford for a home to first double-play, but Virdon's long single to right centerfield scored Hoak and Mazeroski. The Pirates were working their magic.

Yankee pitcher Bobby Shantz took over in the third and blanked the Pirates for five innings, facing only fifteen batters.

In the fifth, Bill Skowron homered off Law, but "The Deacon" did not allow any further scoring. Earlier Murtaugh had said, "All I want from Vern today is five good innings, if he can give me that, I'll have Face and Friend ready."

Murtaugh kept his word after Bobby Richardson singled and Tony Kubek walked to start the sixth inning.

Although his ankle was giving him a lot of trouble, Law felt that with the four-run lead he could win. But Murtaugh went out to the mound and told him, "You have a lot of years left in baseball and I don't want you to risk your arm because you have a bad ankle. Dizzy Dean did it and I don't want it to happen to you."

Danny asked if the ankle was bothering him, but Law shook his head no. However, Don Hoak said he felt the ankle was hindering Law, and that's when Murtaugh signaled for Face.

For the first time in the Series, the Pirates' magnificent relief pitcher didn't have it. He got Roger Maris out on a foul, but a skidding grounder by Mickey Mantle rolled past Dick Groat for a single.

Yogi Berra then hit his eleventh World Series home run high into the second deck in right field, putting the Yankees ahead 5-4.

Then, in the eighth, the Yankees added more when, with two out, Yogi walked, Skowron and Blanchard singled, and Clete Boyer doubled down the left field line.

Bottom of the eighth, Game 7, down 7-4. It was time for the Pirates to go to work.

Gino Cimoli, pinch-hitting for Face, singled to right centerfield. Then came what many call the break of the game. Bill Virdon slashed what appeared to be a routine double-play grounder at Tony Kubek. The ball came up hard, striking Kubek in the throat, knocking him to the ground, stunned.

After Kubek had been lying on the ground for several moments, Casey Stengel ordered him to the bench. Kubek protested, but was replaced by Joe DeMaestri.

When the game continued, Dick Groat singled home Cimoli with a shot to left. After Jim Coates relieved Bobby Shantz, Bob Skinner moved the tying runs up with a sacrifice fly. Both runners held as Nelson flied out, bringing Roberto Clemente to the plate.

Clemente bounced a slow roller toward first. Another routine play except for one thing. No one covered first base. Clemente was safe and Virdon scored.

Up came catcher Hal Smith, only in the game because Smoky Burgess had gone out for a pinch-runner. With the count 2-2, Hal swung and smashed a home run over the left field wall.

Smith leaped and danced around the bases before being greeted by Clemente and Groat who were also jumping with joy.

Casey Stengel, who had earlier gone to the mound to encourage Coates to bear down, went out again. This time he replaced him with Ralph Terry who quickly ended the inning.

The Pirates led 9-7.

But the Yankees were not quite finished. They quickly jumped on Bob Friend with singles from Bobby Richardson and pinch-hitter Dale Long.

Murtaugh wasted no time, bringing in Harvey Haddix. Haddix retired Maris, but Mantle singled to right. Berra then shot a one-bounce smash, grabbed spectacularly by Rocky Nelson who stepped on first base attempting a double-play by tagging Mickey Mantle who was diving back to first. Somehow Mantle dove back in safely and the tying run scored.

Now it was the bottom of the ninth, score tied nine to nine, with number nine, Bill Mazeroski at bat facing Ralph Terry as Art Ditmar warmed up in the Yankee bull pen and Dick Stuart waited in the on-deck circle.

This is how Bill Mazeroski described the at bat: "Nobody told me what to do when I went up to hit in the ninth inning. The score was tied 9-9, and I knew the only important thing was for me to get on somehow."

"I let the first pitch go by. I was waiting for a high fast ball. The second pitch was a fast ball - much like the one I hit for a homer in the first game - and I knew I got good wood on it."

"A cold chill ran down my back a moment after I hit that ball in the ninth inning."

"For a second I didn't know quite what to do. But the message finally got to my legs and I set sail."

"I can't begin to describe how I felt when I saw the ball clear the wall. Time seemed to stand still for an instant."

"Then I ran."

"It was the biggest thrill I ever had. I was so happy I didn't even know what was going through my mind. I do remember when the ball disappeared over the wall. I grabbed my cap and started running. I never thought this would ever happen to me."

"That was some scene when I came into home plate. It looked like half of Forbes Field was there waiting for me. I didn't care though."

"The umpire (Bill Jackowski) cleared a path for me. I made dog-gone sure to touch home plate, though. I wouldn't miss that for the world."

"Getting back to the clubhouse was a real struggle, but I enjoyed every minute of the way. All I could see was a lot of faces in front of me. It reminded me of being downtown on New Year's Eve."

The Pirates were World Champions!

There was a stunned silence in Forbes Field when the bat cracked against the ball and it began its flight toward the left field wall.

Not even the calls of the vendors could be heard. They had all stopped to watch.

The silence lasted until the ball cleared the wall, then Forbes Field exploded.

It seemed as if all 36,683 present burst into cheers and screams. Paper billowed onto the field as confetti rained on the lower boxes.

Fans vaulted over the railings, mobbing the players at home plate.

Outside the park horns began blowing as people danced in the streets, hugging and kissing.

"Destiny's Darlings" had done it!

Game 7
October 13, 1960
Forbes Field
Pittsburgh
Attendance 36,683 Time of Game: 2:36

1st Inning

    YANKEES: Richardson lined to short.
    Kubek popped-up to second.

    Maris fouled-out to Hoak.

    0 Runs 0 Hits 0 Men Left On Base

    PIRATES: Virdon flied to left field.

    Groat popped to short.

    Stuart walked.

    Nelson hit a two run home run into the right field stands.

BEAT 'EM BUCS

Clemente popped-up to second.

2 Runs 1 Hit 0 Men Left On Base Yankees 0 Pirates 2

2nd Inning

YANKEES: Mantle flied to centerfield.

Berra grounded out to third on a good stop by Hoak.

Skowron grounded to short.

0 Runs 0 Hits 0 Men Left On Base

PIRATES: Burgess singled down the first base line into right field.

(Stafford came in to pitch for New York.)

Hoak walked.

Mazeroski bunted a single toward third beating Stafford's throw,

Law grounded into a double-play - Stafford to Blanchard, forcing Burgess - to Skowron.

Virdon singled to right centerfield scoring Hoak as Mazeroski went to second on
Maris' misplay of the hit.

Groat grounded to third.

2 Runs 3 Hits 2 Men Left On Base Yankees 0 Pirates 4

3rd Inning

YABKEES: Blanchard grounded back to the mound.

Boyer popped to second.

Lopez pinch-hit for Stafford and singled to left field.

Richardson flied to left field.

0 Runs 1 Hit 1 man Left On Base

PIRATES: (Shantz came in to pitch for New York.)

Skinner grounded out - Skowron to Shantz.

Nelson walked.

Clemente hit into a double-play - Richardson to Kubek to Skowron.

0 Runs 0 Hits 0 Men Left On Base Yankees 0 Pirates 4

4th Inning

YANKEES: Kubek popped to Groat behind third.

Maris lined to right field.

Mantle singled to right field.

Berra flied to right field.

0 Runs 1 Hit 1 Man Left On Base

PIRATES: Burgess grounded to second.

Virdon grounded to second. HOAK 4-3

Groat lined to the mound. MAZ P6

0 Runs 0 Hits 0 Men Left On Base Yankees 0 Pirates 4

5th Inning

YANKEES: Skowron hit a home run into the lower right field stands.

Blanchard lined to centerfield.

Boyer lined to second.

Shantz popped-up to first.

1 Run 1 Hit 0 Men Left On Base

PIRATES: Law grounded to third.

Virdon grounded to second.

Groat lined to the mound.

0 Runs 0 Hits 0 Men Left On Base Yankees 1 Pirates 4

6th Inning

YANKEES: Richardson singled to centerfield.

Kubek walked.

(Face came in to pitch for Pittsburgh.)

Maris fouled-out to Hoak.

Mantle singled to centerfield scoring Richardson as Kubek went to third.

Berra hit a three-run home run along the foul line into the upper right field stands.

Skowron fouled to Hoak.

Blanchard grounded to first.

3 Runs 3 Hits 0 Men Left On Base

PIRATES: Skinner flied to right field.

Nelson grounded out - Skowron to Shantz.

Clemente bounced back to the mound.

0 Runs 0 Hits 0 Men Left On Base Yankees 5 Pirates 4

7th Inning

YANKEES: Boyer flied to centerfield.

Shantz bounced a single over Hoak's head.

Richardson forced Shantz at second - Hoak to Mazeroski.

Kubek lined to right field.

0 Runs 1 Hit 1 man Left On Base

PIRATES: Burgess singled to centerfield.

Christopher came in to run for Burgess.

Hoak lined to left field.

Mazeroski grounded into a double-play - Kubek to Richardson to Skowron.

0 Runs 1 Hit 0 Men Left On Base Yankees 5 Pirates 4

8th Inning

YANKEES: (Smith came in to catch for Pittsburgh.)

Maris grounded to the mound.
Mantle lined to short.
BERRA WALK
Skowron singled on a high bouncing ball to third as Berra went to second.

Blanchard singled to right centerfield scoring Berra and sending Skowron to third.
Boyer doubled into the left field corner scoring Skowron as Blanchard stopped at third.

Shantz flied to right field.

2 Runs 3 Hits 2 Men Left On Base

PIRATES: Cimoli pinch-hit for Face and singled to right centerfield.

Virdon hit a bad hop single that hit Kubek in the throat.

Cimoli stopped at second.

(DeMaestri replaced Kubek at shortstop for New York.)

Groat singled past third scoring Cimoli as Virdon went to third.

(Coates came in to pitch for New York.)

Skinner sacrificed up both runners.- Boyer to Skowron.

Nelson flied to right field - the runners held.

Clemente singled on a slow chopper to first scoring Virdon as Groat moved to third.

Smith hit a three-run home run over the left field wall.

(Terry came in to pitch for New York.)

Hoak flied to left field.

5 Runs 5 Hits 0 Men Left On Base. Yankees 7 Pirates 9

BEAT 'EM BUCS

9th Inning

YANKEES: (Friend came in to pitch for Pittsburgh.)

Richardson singled to left centerfield.

Long pinch-hit for DeMaestri and singled to right moving Richardson to second.

(Haddix came in to pitch for Pittsburgh.)

Maris fouled-out to Smith.

Mantle singled to right centerfield scoring Richardson and sending Long to third.

McDougald came in to run for Long.

Berra grounded to first scoring McDougald as mantle moved to second.

Skowron forced Berra - Groat to Mazeroski.

2 Runs 3 Hits 1 Man Left On Base

PIRATES: (McDougald playing third - Boyer shifts to shortstop.)

Mazeroski hit Terry's second pitch over the left field wall.

1 Run 1 Hit 0 Men Left On Base

FINAL SCORE: Yankees 9 Pirates 10

FINANCIAL FIGURES

GAME ONE
Attendance - 36,676
Total Receipts (net) - $233,260.24
Commissioner's Share - $34,989.40
Player Pool - $118,962.72
Pittsburgh Club's Share - $19,827.12
New York Club's Share - $19,827.12
American League's Share - $19,827.12
National League's Share - $19,927.12

GAME TWO
Attendance - 37,308
Total Receipts (net) - $236,765.13
Commissioner's Share - $35,364.77
Player Pool - $120,240.22
Pittsburgh Club's Share - $20,040.04
New York Club's Share - $20,040.04
American League's Share - $20.040.03
National League's Share - $20,040.03

GAME THREE
Attendance - 70,001
Total Receipts (net) - $436,587.88
Commissioner's Share - $65,488.18
Player Pool - $222,659.82
Pittsburgh Club's Share - $37,109.97
New York Club's Share - $37,109.97
American League's Share - $37,109.97
National League's Share - $37,109.97

GAME FOUR
Attendance - 67,812
Total Receipts (net) - $431,925.60
Commissioner's Share - $64,788.84
Player Pool - $220,282.06
Pittsburgh Club's Share - $36,713.68
New York Club's Share - $36,713.68
American League's Share - $36,713.67
National League's Share - $35,713.67

GAME FIVE
Attendance - 62,753
Total Receipts (net) - $240,529.40
Commissioner's Share - $62,870.32
Pittsburgh Club's Share - $89,066.28
New York Club's Share - $89,066.28
American League's Share - $89,066.28
National League's Share -$89,066.28

GAME SIX
Attendance - 38,580
Total Receipts (net) - $240,529.40
Commissioner's Share - $36,079.41
Pittsburgh Club's Share - $51,112.50
New York Club's Share - $51,112.50
American League's Share - $51,112.50
National League's Share - $51,112.50

GAME SEVEN
Attendance - 36,683
Total Receipts (net) - $233,424.19
Commissioner's Share - $35,013.63
Pittsburgh Club's Share - $49,062.64

New York Club's Share - $49,062.64
American League's Share - $49,062.64
National League's Share - $49,062.64

SEVEN GAME TOTALS
Attendance - 349,813
Total Receipts (net) - $2,230,627.88
Commissioner's Share - $344,594.19
Player Pool (First four games only) - $682, 144.82
Pittsburgh Club's Share - $303,472.23
New York Club's Share - $303,472.23
American League's Share - $303,472.20
National League's Share - $303,472.21

CHAPTER 12
We Had 'em All The Way: Fan and Player Reactions

Unlike the situation in the locker room in Milwaukee, where the celebrating was slow getting started due to the fact that the Pirates had lost the game but won the National League pennant, the celebrating began in earnest almost immediately. Gino Cimoli alternated cries of, "Nine big ones ($9,000 was the winner's share), boys - in the kick! Nine big ones, with, "They broke all the records, but we won the game!"

General manager Joe L. Brown handed Mazeroski a champagne bottle. Maz took one swallow and made a face. Meanwhile, coach Frank Oceak climbed on a chair and showered Brown with beer.

Rocky Nelson, a cigar in his hand, reflected on the game. "Smith hit the big blow that won the game for us," he said. "No doubt about it. Maz's hit was anti-climactic to me."

Gino Cimoli continued his antics, pouring champagne over Danny Murtaugh's head as the Buc manager was being interviewed. Soaked, but happy, Murtaugh, in his usual dead-pan manner, quipped, "Only time in the Series we scored a lot of runs, and we needed every one of them, didn't we?"

When someone yelled, "Pirate Power!", Hal Smith joked back, "We don't have any power - remember?"

Pirate owners John Galbreath and Tom Johnson moved from player to player shaking hands and offering congratulations with voices hoarse from yelling.

Seventy-four year old Bill McKecknie, the last Pirate manager to win a World Series, was beaming. "I'm glad I lived long enough to see something like this," he commented to reporters.

Many of the players began throwing wet towels around the locker room. One hit Joe L. Brown in the face, and another, thrown by pitcher George Witt, struck Tom Cheney on the neck.

"Witt," Chaney yelled, "You never threw that straight in your life."

Writers drifted from locker to locker as the players continued to shake hands with anybody in sight and pop champagne corks.

While the champagne and beer flowed, and the wet towels flew, Bob Friend stood silently by his locker.

A writer assured him that the celebration was just as much his as the other players, but Friend replied that he didn't feel that way. He suggested that the reporter get his story from the guys who did it. Friend then turned away and sat by himself in front of his locker.

Although he had lost the two Series games he had started, and had been ineffective as a reliever in the seventh game, he had won 18 games during the regular season. But for Bob Friend, that didn't seem to be enough.

In the Yankee locker room most of the players just sat at their lockers. They seemed too stunned to realize that the Pirates were the World Champions for the first time in thirty-five years.

Rookie, Johnny Blanchard, who caught games six and seven while Yogi Berra played the outfield and Elston Howard sat on the bench with a fractured hand, sit in front of his locker, head in his hands, sobbing.

There was an air of sorrow and dejection. Many players, including Mantle and Skowron, sat silently facing their lockers.

When Roger Maris asked Yogi Berra, "What happened?",

Yogi replied, "We just got beat, Roger, by the damndest baseball team that me or you or anybody else ever played against."

Casey Stengel kept undressing as he talked to a handful of reporters. "Pitching beat me in the last game, not my infielders or outfielders," he emphasized to the writers. "But still we came back twice. "These boys fought and I told 'em so, too."

"I think it was remarkable what they did."

When asked what he said to his players, Casey responded, "They have no reason in the world to be ashamed."

"A fighting team...that's what they were and I told them so. Keep your heads held high, boys, I told them."

"You deserved it."

"They kept fighting right through the ninth inning, Stengel said, putting a strong emphasis on the word "fighting."

As the celebrating in the Pirate clubhouse began to wind down, Oakland and the city of Pittsburgh were still going strong. Players trying to get to their cars had a variety of different experiences.

Smoky Burgess quietly left Forbes Field and made his way through the melee to a Forbes Street parking lot where he reached his car without a single person recognizing him. But police had to rescue Hal Smith from a mob of autograph seekers when he arrived at an Oakland parking lot after the game to pick up his car. "Your car is over here," said a policeman. The officer then shoved Smith into a large black Cadillac. As the crowd surrounded the car, Hal appeared to be trying to say something, but no one seemed to notice. "O. K., Hal," the policeman said. "Take her away."

Smith responded, "Officer, this isn't my car!"

The scene with the crowd was repeated as Smith was finally pushed into another nearby car. This time it was the right vehicle.

Inching slowly down Bouquet Street in his station wagon, ElRoy Face finally reached a policeman attempting to direct traffic in front of the main entrance to Forbes Field.

Face was hoping to travel straight to escape autograph seekers, but the officer wanted him to make a right turn.

Not recognizing Face, the policeman kept signaling for him to make a right hand turn. As ElRoy continued going straight, the officer yelled, "Hey buddy, this is a crowded ballpark. What's the matter…don't you know your way around here?"

At 3:36:30 Bill Mazeroski hit the home run that won the 1960 world championship. Within seconds, horns began sounding downtown and paper began pouring from office building windows.

Confetti and paper was knee-deep on Fifth and Forbes Avenues as office workers, shoppers and fans joined in the yelling and cheering. Within an hour and a half, happy Pirate fans and groups of people going nowhere in particular had halter traffic on almost all downtown Pittsburgh streets.

The bars were jammed as patrons toasted the Pirate victory, often carrying their drinks with them out into the street.

A group of police tried to move a street car up Fifth Avenue by walking in front of it as it inched forward, but gave up when the jubilant crowd refused to move.

Day shift police were ordered to remain in the city indefinitely to handle the huge traffic jams in Oakland and downtown.

The biggest celebration was in the heart of the Golden Triangle where veteran policemen said they never had seen a celebration to equal what was happening - not even on VE and VJ Days during World War II. Street cars and busses on Fifth Avenue were backed-up from Wood Street to Sixth Avenue as helpless police took everything in relatively good spirit.

One policeman said: "This is the worst thing that has ever happened to me - but I'm kidding. I love it."

Many teenagers climbed all over street cars and busses ripping Pirate banners from utility poles.

Employees at the Hilton Hotel moved every piece of breakable furniture out of the lobby as soon as the game ended.

A Hilton official, William Steele, said, "This place will be a madhouse."

The celebration pick up in intensity when office workers who hadn't deserted their offices right after the game joined the festivities.

Allegheny County police had put 32 mounted police on stand-by in case they were needed to control the crowd. And by 5:30 about 500 city policemen were on duty.

Caught in Oakland in the traffic jam after the game, Safety Director Rosenberg could only communicate by radio. Superintendent James W. Slusser was also limited to radio communication.

Back in Oakland the celebration moved from outside Forbes Field to the Schenley Apartments of the University of Pittsburgh. There were thousands of pirate fans milling in the area. Two clergymen could be seen walking down the street waving Pirate banners and wearing pirate hats.

One policeman, obviously of Polish descent yelled to the crowd, "It took a Polish boy (Mazeroski) to do it!"

Crowds yelled, traffic stalled, confetti rained and church bells rang, because Pirate fans all knew, in the words of Pirate announcer Bob Prince, "WE HAD 'EM ALL THE WAY!"

CHAPTER 13
DID THE BETTER TEAM LOSE?

At the conclusion of Game 7 of the 1960 World Series the media was filled with quotes from Yankee players bemoaning the fact that they had been beaten. Time after time the phrase "The better team lost." could be heard. On the morning of the final game, Yogi Berra complained: "I just don't understand it, we know we're a better ball club." After the game Roger Maris fumed: "The Pirates should never beat our club. They were real lucky." He was echoed by Dale Long, who snapped: "The best team lost. Imagine Hal Smith hitting a homer." (Smith hit 8 more homers than Long in the 1960 season.) Perhaps that was why the Pirates were able to come out on top after seven games. They took their beatings, but they weren't intimidated by the Yankees.. Unlike the Yankees, they knew they were a good team without having to constantly tell everyone. Danny Murtaugh was quoted as remarking that it wasn't how many runs you scored, but the number of games won that determined the winner of the championship.

The Yankees did indeed have a long and illustrious history following them into the 1960 World Series, but it was the 1960 team playing the Pirates, not the ghosts of champions past. With that kind of history it seems odd that the "we should have won" attitude prevailed. You don't win championships with "would have," "could have," or "should have." You play your best and take both victory and defeat with dignity.

The Pirates were no match statistic-wise for the Yankees in the Series, but if the 1960 seasons of both teams are compared it becomes quite evident that the teams were on equal footing, and that in some areas, the Pirates performed better than the Yankees.

Beginning with their win - loss totals, the Pirates were 95-59 (.617) leading the National League by 7 games, the Yankees 97-57 (.630) winning it by 8 games. In their respective leagues,

Pittsburgh led in runs scored (734), fewest runs scored by opponents (593), doubles (236), and batting average (.276). They were second in triples and slugging average. Fielding placed them in second with fewest errors, tied with fielding average, and in the lead with 163 double plays.

Pitching saw them with the fewest walks (386), and third in shutouts and E.R.A.

In the American League, the Yankees were first with 746 runs scored, 193 home runs, and a .426 slugging average. Their pitching led the league with 16 shutouts, 42 saves, they tied Baltimore with a league leading E.R.A. of 3.52.

1960 Season Statistics

	W	L	Pct.	GA	R	OR	SB	2B	3B	HR	Avg.	S. Avg.
Pirates	95	59	.617	7	**734**	**593**	34	**236**	56	120	**.276**	.407
Yankees	97	57	.630	8	**746**	627	37	215	49	**193**	.260	**.426**

(Bold Print - Led League)

A look at the statistics of the starting line-ups and the main pitchers shows some more interesting comparisons.

Comparisons are arguable since we are talking about two different leagues with the players facing different competition, but on a man to man match-up the figures are very interesting. At first base Skowron had the higher average, but home runs and RBIs were very close. Mazeroski at second performed much better than Richardson (Although Bobby made up for his hitting in the Series!). Groat was MVP and won the batting title, but Kubek hit with more power. Don Hoak at third gets the edge with a higher average and RBI production. Maris was the American League MVP in right field, but Clemente had the superior average and was only 18 RBIs behind Roger even though Roberto had 23 fewer home runs. Mantle versus Virdon? With all due respect to Virdon's spectacular fielding, no contest. The left field battle goes to Skinner. Lopez hit for a higher average, but Skinner had twice the RBIs and 6 more homers.

If we combine the two catchers used by each team, New York's combo has 17 more RBIs, but the Bucs hit 34 points higher.

Starting Line-up Statistics

	Avg.	HR	RBI
1st Base			
Dick Stuart	.260	23	83
Bill Skowron	.309	26	91
2nd Base			
Bill Mazeroski	.273	11	64
Bobby Richardson	.252	1	26
Shortstop			
Dick Groat	.325	2	50
Tony Kubek	.273	14	62
3rd Base			
Don Hoak	.282	16	79
Clete Boyer	.242	14	46

Right Field			
Roberto Clemente	.316	16	94
Roger Maris	.283	39	112
Centerfield			
Bill Virdon	.264	8	40
Mickey Mantle	.275	40	94
Left Field			
Bob Skinner	.273	15	86
Hector Lopez	.284	9	42
Catcher			
Smoky Burgess	.294	7	39
Hal Smith	.295	11	45
Yogi Berra	.276	15	62
Elston Howard	.245	6	39
Pirates Combined	.294	18	84
Yankees Combined	.260	21	101

When it comes to pitching, if we use the top five winning pitchers from each squad, the Pirates are 72-44 with an E.R.A. of 3.33, and the Yankees come in at 59-32 with a 3.36 E.R.A.

Top Five Pitchers' Statistics

	W	L	E.R.A.
Vernon Law	20	9	3.08
Bob Friend	18	12	3.00
Harvey Haddix	11	10	3.97
Vinegar Bend Mizell	13	5	3.12
ElRoy Face	10	8	2.90
Art Ditmar	15	9	3.06
Jim Coates	13	3	4.28
Whitey Ford	12	9	3.08
Ralph Terry	10	8	3.40
Bob Turley	9	3	3.27
Pirates Combined	72	44	3.33
Yankees Combined	59	32	3.36

All in all, quite an interesting comparison.

Would the Yankees have dominated the Pirates as they did in the World Series if they had played in the same league together? Does the atmosphere of post-season play affect players' performances? Is this why Bobby Richardson became a force to be reckoned with and made Bob Friend less effective than he had been all season? Does luck play a role?

We will never know, but one thing is certain. No matter how it was done, the Pirates finished with 4 wins and the 1960 World Championship.

1960
Pittsburgh Pirates
Awards and Honors

Roberto Clemente - MOST POPULAR PIRATE
Presented by the Joseph Horne Co., after a poll of district fans.

Bob Friend - COMEBACK OF THE YEAR
Presented annually by United Press International to the baseball player who has come back with a good season after a disappointing one.

Dick Groat - MOST VALUABLE PLAYER AWARD
Presented annually by the Baseball Writers Association of America for the most valuable player in each major league.

THE SILVER BAT
Presented annually by the Hillerich and Bradsby Co., to the batting champion of each major league.

THE LOU GEHRIG AWARD
Presented annually by the Phi Delta Theta fraternity to the major league player who most exemplifies the character of Lou Gehrig both on and off the playing field.

THE DAPPER DAN AWARD
Presented annually by the Dapper Dan Club of Pittsburgh to the sports personality who did the most to publicize Pittsburgh in the past year.

MOST VALUABLE PLAYER AWARD
Presented by the Joseph Horne Co., after a poll of Pittsburgh fans.

Harvey Haddix - GOLD GLOVE AWARD
Presented annually by the Rawlings Manufacturing Co., to the best fielders in the American and national League as chosen by a position vote of their opposing players.

Don Hoak - HARVEY J. BOYLE MEMORIAL AWARD
Presented annually by the Pittsburgh Chapter of the baseball Writers Association of America to the outstanding figure in Pittsburgh sports, the previous year.

Vernon Law - CY YOUNG AWARD
Presented annually by the Baseball Writers Association of America to the outstanding pitcher in the major leagues.

LOS ANGELES AWARD
Presented annually by the local Chapter of Baseball Writers Association of America for outstanding baseball achievement.

Bill Mazeroski - PLAYER-OF-THE-YEAR
Presented annually by *The Sporting News* to the major league player who has done the most outstanding job the previous year.

BABE RUTH AWARD
Presented annually by the New York Chapter of the Baseball Writers Association of America to the outstanding player in the previous year's World Series.

GOLD GLOVE AWARD
Presented annually by the Rawlings Manufacturing Co., to the best fielder in the American and National League as chosen by a position vote of their opposing players.

WORLD SERIES HERO AWARD
Presented annually by the Chicago Chapter of the Baseball Writers Association of America to the outstanding player in the previous year's World Series.

PENNSYLVANIA ATHLETE-OF-THE-YEAR
Presented by the Pennsylvania Railroad.

Danny Murtaugh - MANAGER-OF-THE-YEAR
Presented annually by *The Sporting News* to the major league manager who has done the most outstanding job the previous year.

NATIONAL LEAGUE MANAGER OF THE YEAR
Presented annually by the Associated Press in a poll of AP sportswriters.

NATIONAL LEAGUE MANAGER-OF-THE-YEAR
Presented annually by the United Press international in a poll of UPI sportswriters.

THE ACHIEVEMENT OF THE YEAR
For leading the Pirates to the World Championship. Presented annually by the Chicago Chapter of the Baseball Writers Association of America for the outstanding sports' achievement of the year.

MILWAUKEE AWARD
Presented by the Milwaukee Chapter of the Baseball Writers Association of America for World Series victory.

CHAPTER 14
WE STILL HONOR AND REMEMBER: THE MAZEROSKI WALL

The memory of Bill Mazeroski's ninth inning game winning home run continues to be celebrated every October 13th by die-hard Pirate fans at the one remaining section of the ivy-covered brick wall of Forbes Field. Embedded in the sidewalk across the street, near the entrance to the University of Pittsburgh's Forbes Quadrangle, are red bricks which outline where the rest of the wall once stood. There is also a plaque which identifies where Maz's home run went over the left field wall. Inside the building, under a protective sheet of glass, is home plate. Not THE home plate, that one was dug up by Michael "Red" Sipa of Squirrel Hill during the frenzied celebration after Game Seven,. But grown men have been seen sliding, in coats and ties, down the hallway and across the facsimile.

The ritual began one beautiful October day in 1985, when Saul Finkelstein decided it might be nice to go to the wall and listen to a tape of Chuck Thompson calling the play-by play of the final game of the 1960 World Series to commemorate the 25th anniversary of the Pirates' victory and Maz's home run. Saul did not attend the final game, but he had been at home listening to it on the radio. When the Pirates fell behind, he decided it might be a good time to bury his cat which had died the night before. After putting his pet to rest in his back yard, he returned to hear the Pirates pull it out and win the championship. On that October day in 1985, many passer-bys looked at Saul in surprise, and a few even stopped briefly, but it was basically a solitary vigil, with Saul timing it so that the tape ended at just about the moment when Mazeroski hit the home run.

Gradually the word got around that Saul was commemorating the victory, and a few other fans began to join him at the wall. Crowds averaged about twenty to forty people, with fans bringing ticket stubs, programs, photographs and other memorabilia to share as they listened to the game. They dutifully removed their hats and stood quietly or sing as the National Anthem was played, cheered when the Pirates made a good play or got a crucial hit, cringed when the Yankees scored, and finally cheered and patted each other on the back when Maz hit Terry's 0-1 pitch over the left field wall as Yogi Berra helplessly watched. One fan even tries to wager a bet every year, after the Yankees tie it up, that the Bucs will somehow pull it out, but so far no one has taken him up on it.

Occasionally former Pirates attend the festivities. Bob Friend is a regular, as are Nellie King, Nellie Briles and ElRoy Face. The 40th anniversary in 2000 brought a very special guest to the wall. Around about the eighth inning, the crowd, which was much larger than usual (several hundred due to it being the 40th anniversary), was surprised to see a white stretch limo pull up to the curb. Exiting from the back seat, a little grayer and a little heavier, but still with a familiar twinkle in his eye, was Bill Mazeroski. At that moment something very special happened. The crowd broke into a warm round of applause. No pushing or shoving, but instead a respectful exhibition of admiration and thanks. Maz slowly made his way to the short brick wall that separates the sidewalk from the actual wall, shaking hands and talking as he went. He sat down next to the tape player and a variety of pictures and memorabilia to listen to the conclusion of the game. As we all waited, he patiently and neatly signed every article that was passed to him. Once again, there was calmness about the group. Strangers politely and carefully passed treasured items to Maz for him to sign and then, just as carefully, passed the items back to their owners.

Finally, it was the bottom of the 9th. Maz got up and was joined by King, Friend and Briles in front of the tape player. Terry threw the first pitch. Ball one. The crowd grew restless. The next pitch was described in almost silence, but when Chuck Thompson told us it was a home run and the Pirates were champs, the crowd went wild. All of the former Pirates gave high fives and thumbs-up among what seemed to be a celebration just as loud as the one recorded on the tape 40 years earlier. Suddenly everyone was forty years younger.

Eventually the crowd began to quiet down and Maz moved through the crowd (still signing autograph and shaking hands) and got into the limo. He pulled away to another round of cheers and applause. The crowd then began to quietly disperse. A few people took photographs of the wall, while others tried to get up a game in a small ballpark behind the wall named, quite appropriately, Bill Mazeroski Field.

The feelings that the fans have for Bill Mazeroski and the other 1960 Pirate players is quite unlike that for other Pittsburgh championship teams. I have been fortunate to have experienced the two Pirate championships in 1971 and 1979, and have been at numerous events where players from those teams were present, but the fans react to the '60 Bucs in a much more personal way. The players also seem to have the same feelings for the '60 fans. When asked why there is such a bond, Cy Young winner Vernon Law responded: "My own personal opinion is, the city hadn't had a winner for a long time, and we came along and finally put it together and won. But, by the same token, we had a bunch of guys that were community oriented. I know I was out in the community all the time giving speaking engagements, promoting the game and that sort of thing. They related more to us. We were like the blue collar workers back then. I really think for that reason alone is the reason why they relate more to us than some of the other guys." Hal Smith reacted similarly: "I think it was because it was thirty five years since they had even been in a World Series, and people got behind us. They watched the team come from behind so many times that the whole city got behind us. In fact, the whole state, everybody did. We got to know a lot of the people."

When asked about the 1960 Series, and Maz's home run, fans old enough to remember can tell you stories that have become family legends. The same doesn't seem to be true of the other championships. Some say it is merely nostalgia, the natural thing that happens when fans get older and are distanced from the events. Perhaps, but it has been almost thirty years since the '71 championship and I have yet to see groups of fans playing tapes of Game Seven and celebrating every year. Some believe it is because the '71 and '79 teams won on the road in Baltimore, but whatever the reason, the 1960 Pirates will always hold a special place in the hearts of Pirate fans and as long as the wall still stands in Oakland, they will celebrate every October 13th.

AFTERWORD

Looking back on the 1960 Pittsburgh Pirates and the championship season now, over fifty years later, it is easy to see was the team was labeled as *Destiny's Darlings*. It seemed to be the team's destiny to win the pennant and championship.

All season long and into the World Series they found a way to win. An attitude pervaded the entire team that they couldn't be beaten. Time after time in the late innings someone would become the hero. Even after losing 16-3, 10-0 and 12-0 to the mighty Yankees, they still won. Catcher Hal Smith put it into perspective when asked how manager Danny Murtaugh and the team reacted after the humiliating losses. "Danny never got down on us. He'd simply say, 'Go out and get them next time.' We didn't feel we could get beat." Pitcher Vernon Law echoed the sentiment. "Danny was never hard on us after the big losses. We'd just put it behind us and come out the next day ready to win."

However it did take a little more than a positive attitude to produce the championship. In researching the season and the Series I was constantly made aware of how the Pirates were able to play good, sound, fundamental baseball. When necessary they could lay down bunts. In one game they loaded the bases with three consecutive bunt base hits. Intentional walks played an important role, especially in the World Series. In several of the Series games the bat was literally taken out of Mickey Mantle's hands when he received intentional passes. It seems as though today that concept has been lost. Too many times we see pitchers, particularly relievers "challenging" the hitters rather than recognizing the potential threat and issuing the pass.

There was also the prevalent work ethic of finishing what you started. In the words of Yogi Berra, "It ain't over 'til it's over." Even in losses it wasn't unusual to see pitchers with complete games. Of the four Pirate starters, Vernon Law tied Warren Spahn for the League lead with 18, Bob Friend was close behind in second place with 16, Vinegar Bend Mizell had 8, and Harvey Haddix was low man with 4. That's a total of 46 complete games from starters alone. Check the box scores for low hit games. There were quite a few games with fewer than 7 hits.

Before we start excusing these facts with the reduction of the height of the pitcher's mound and other changes that penalized the batters, let's take a look at the batting statistics. Both the American and the National League had identical composite batting averages of .255, with the Pirates hitting at a .276 pace. Dick Groat led the National League with a .325 mark and Pete Runnels mastered the American League hitting .320. Twelve Pirates hit above .260, with 6 at .290 or better, including Dick Groat (.325), Roberto Clemente (.314), Dick Schofield (.333), Rocky Nelson (.300), Hal Smith (.295), and Smoky Burgess (.294). The hitters *were* hitting.

Whatever the reasons, the 1960 Pittsburgh were a very special team. They played fundamentally sound, exciting baseball that enabled them to succeed when just about everyone predicted failure. They truly were *Destiny's Darlings*.

APPENDIX A
1960 Pittsburgh Pirate Player Profiles / Statistics

The Manager

Daniel "Danny" Murtaugh   **#40**
Danny Murtaugh broke into professional baseball in 1937, making the majors with the Philadelphia Phillies in 1941. He remained with the Phillies until he entered military service in 1944. When Danny was discharged in 1946, he found himself the property of Rochester in the International League. Murtaugh played second base alongside shortstop Eddie Joost. Their keystone combination was one of the best that year. Joost entered the majors with the Philadelphia Athletics in 1947, but in spite of his .322 average, Danny remained in the minors. Playing for Milwaukee in the American Association that year, he led to Brewers to the pennant, victory in the playoffs, and in the little World Series. Murtaugh joined the Pirates in 1948, and as an aggressive, hustling, smooth-fielding second baseman helped them come from nowhere to almost win the National League pennant that year.

Danny started managing in 1952 with the Pirates' farm team in New Orleans leading the Pelicans for three years. In 1955, he managed Charleston, West Virginia. He became a Pirate coach in 1956, and continued in that capacity until being named manager on August 3, 1957, replacing Bobby Bragan. From the time Murtaugh took over the helm until the end of the season, the Pirates played .510 baseball. Even so, the team wound up in seventh place. In 1958, Danny's first full year as manager, the Pirates were the "Cinderella" team of baseball, finishing second and earning him the "Manager of the Year" award.

One injury after another hampered the Pirates and Murtaugh in the 1959 season. That year the Pirates hosted one of the All Star games on July 7th at Forbes Field, with the National League winning 5-4 before 35,277 fans, and the city of Pittsburgh was celebrating its' bicentennial. But the team lost Gene Baker before the season ever started, got no wins from George Witt and Curt Raydon, who had 17 victories between them as rookie sensations in 1958, and saw catcher Hank Foiles and right fielder Roberto Clemente on the disabled list for a month each. Even so, the Pirates were only four games out of first place going into September. They eventually came in fourth.

Danny entered 1960 confident that he had a contending club. He felt that when all of the players were playing up to their potential, they did not have an outstanding weakness in the line-up. In his opinion they had good defense, adequate team speed and were a pretty good hitting team. The 1960 team proved him right and helped him to earn the League's Manager of the Year Award for the second time in three years.

The Coaches

George Sisler - BATTING COACH
Although he was given the official title of "Special Assistant to the Manager," Hall of Fame first baseman George Sisler was

the Pirates' batting coach. Although all major league clubs now have batting coaches, when Sisler was appointed one on a full time basis in 1957, he was the first one.

Sisler hit over .400 twice as a St. Louis Brown. He hit .407 in 1920, and .420 in 1922, and was one of the all-time finest first basemen. He began as a pitcher at the University of Michigan under coach Branch Rickey, and broke into the majors with the Browns as a pitcher. One of his pitching highlights was a 1-0 shutout over Washington's Walter Johnson. Rickey converted him into a first baseman, a position he played for the rest of his career. Sisler was also playing manager of the Browns for three years.

James "Mickey" Vernon - First Base Coach   #42

A veteran of 17 years in the majors as a first baseman, Mickey was the Pirates first base coach. Mickey spent most of his time with the Washington Senators, whom he joined in 1939. He also played with the Red Sox, Cleveland, and Milwaukee.

Vernon is a life-long friend of manager Danny Murtaugh. They were both born and raised in a suburb of Philadelphia, and they were teammates on the Chester, Pennsylvania American Legion team in 1934 and 1935.

Mickey played on six American League All Star teams, won the American League batting title in 1946 hitting .353 and again in 1953 with a .337 mark. On four occasions he led American League first basemen in fielding. He also played in 9 games for the Pirates in 1960.

William "Bill" Burwell - Pitching Coach   #41

Bill Burwell first became the Pirates' pitching coach in 1958. He has served the Pittsburgh Pirates as a player, coach, scout, minor league manager, managerial consultant and advisor in his long career.

After World War I, he pitched for the St. Louis Browns, and then spent 15 years in the American Association with Columbus, Indianapolis, Minneapolis, and Louisville. Returning to the majors with Pittsburgh in 1928, he stayed until 1933, when he returned to managing and coaching. He managed Louisville to a Little World Series victory in 1939, and managed the Pirates for a brief time in 1947 after Billy Herman had been fired.

Samuel "Sam" Narron - Bull Pen Coach   #43

Sam Narron began serving the Pirates as their bull pen coach in 1952. As a catcher, he played with the St. Louis Cardinals in 1935, 1942 and 1943, including an appearance in the 1943 World Series for St. Louis.

Narron was with the Brooklyn Dodger organization from 1944 through 1949, before joining them as a coach, a position he held until joining the Pirates coaching staff.

Frank Oceak - Third Base Coach   #44

Frank Oceak has served as the Pirates third base coach since 1958. Until joining the coaching staff, Oceak was the Pittsburgh organization's oldest minor league manager in the point of continuous service. He began managing Pirate farm clubs in 1942.

Frank started managing in 1938, after a career as a second baseman, winning his first minor league pennant in 1939, with the Fayette, Arkansas team.

Leonard "Lenny" Levy - Coach and Batting Practice Aid #45

Serving as a coach and batting practice aid at home games, Lenny Levy also was a scout throughout the Tri-State area during the summer. Having an automobile agency a few blocks from Forbes Field limited him to part-time duty with the Pirates.

Lenny was a Pirate coach under managers Pie Traynor and Frankie Frisch from 1938 through 1942. He served with the United states Marines during World War II, and returned to baseball when he was discharged.

Virgil Trucks - Batting Practice Pitcher   #10

A veteran American League pitcher, Virgil Trucks joined the Pirates as a batting practice pitcher midway through the 1960 season.

Most of Trucks' 17 year Major League career was spent with the Detroit Tigers, but he also played for the St. Louis Browns, Chicago White Sox and Kansas City A's.

Virgil pitched six no-jitters in professional baseball, two in the majors. Both of his major league no-hitters came in 1952 while he was with the Tigers. The first one was against the Washington Senators on May 15, and the other was against the New York Yankees on August 25, in Yankee Stadium.

Eugene Walter Baker - Infielder   #16

Born on June 15, 1925, at Davenport, Iowa. Bats right. Throws right. Height - 6-1. Weight 170. How obtained - Traded to Pittsburgh with Dee Fondy from Chicago Cubs for Dale Long and Lee Walls, May 1, 1957.

Gene Baker began his baseball career on the Davenport, Iowa sandlots. After time in the service, he played for the Kansas City Monarchs before moving on to the Chicago Cubs organization where he played for Springfield, Des Moines and Los Angeles before becoming the first African-American to play for the parent Cubs in 1953.

After a one and a half year lay-off due to an injured knee, Baker saw limited action in 1960. He was used primarily as a pinch hitter and pinch runner.

YEAR	CLUB	LEAGUE	G	AB	R	H	2B	3B	HR	RBI	AVG.
				RECORDS							
1960	Pittsburgh	National	33	37	5	9	0	0	0	4	.243
				WORLD SERIES							
1960	Pittsburgh	National	3	3	0	0	0	0	0	0	.000

Richard Anthony Barone - Infielder   #48

Born on October 13, 1932 at San Jose, California. Bats and throws right. Height - 5-9. Weight - 165. How obtained - Product of Pittsburgh Farm System.

Dick Barone lettered in baseball and basketball at San Jose High School. He began as a pitcher, but switched to the infield his senior year.

Ben Fontaine, the Pirates' west coast scout, signed Dick at a tryout camp in Anaheim in 1951. He has played for the Pirate farm teams in Great Falls, Billings, Williamsport, New Orleans, Columbus and Salt Lake City.

Dick came up to the Pirates late in the 1960 season and filled in at shortstop. He appeared in only three games.

			RECORDS							
YEAR	CLUB	LEAGUE	G	AB	R	H	2B	3B	HR	RBI	AVG.
1960	Pittsburgh	National	3	6	0	0	0	0	0	0	.000

Harry James Bright - Infielder #8

Born on September 22, 1929 at Kansas City, Missouri. Bats and throws right. Height - 6. Weight - 190. How obtained - Purchased from Sacramento of the Pacific Coast League.

Harry Bright began his career in 1946 with Twin Falls in the pioneer League. In 1949 he led the K-M-O League in RBIs, and with Clovis in 1950, he led the league with a .413 batting average.

Harry got into four games as a pinch hitter in 1960, but was hitless.

			RECORDS							
YEAR	CLUB	LEAGUE	G	AB	R	H	2B	3B	HR	RBI	AVG.
1960	Pittsburgh	National	4	4	0	0	0	0	0	0	.000

Forrest Harrill Burgess - Catcher #6

Born on February 6, 1927 at Caroleen, North Carolina. Bats left. Throws left. Height - 5-8. Weight - 187. How obtained - Traded to Pittsburgh with Harvey Haddix and Don Hoak from Cincinnati on January 31, 1959, for Frank Thomas, Whammy Douglas, Jim Pendleton and Johnny Powers.

Smokey began his baseball career in 1944 with the Chicago Cubs organization, making the majors with them in 1949. Before coming to Pittsburgh he spent time with the Phillies and Reds.

Recognized as one of the best natural hitters in the game, he was noted for coming off the bench cold at anytime and more often than not getting a hit. He rarely went into a slump.

In 1960, Smokey caught most of the time when a righthander faced the Pirates being platooned by Danny Murtaugh with Hal Smith, a righthanded hitter. Burgess was the clubs best pinch hitter with a .450 average in 24 games, and for the first time in his career he led all National League catchers in fielding with a .994 percentage. He also made his fourth appearance as a National League All Star.

YEAR	CLUB	LEAGUE	G	RECORDS AB	R	H	2B	3B	HR	RBI	AVG.
1960	Pittsburgh	National	110	337	33	99	15	2	7	39	.294
1960	Pittsburgh	National	2	ALL STAR GAME 3	0	0	0	0	0	0	.000
1960	Pittsburgh	National	5	WORLD SERIES 18	2	6	1	0	0	0	.333

Thomas Edgar Cheney - Pitcher #34

Born on October 14, 1935 at Morgan, Georgia. Bats and throws right. Height - 6.

Weight - 180. How obtained - Traded to Pittsburgh with Gino Cimoli from St. Louis for pitcher Ronnie Kline, December 21, 1959.

Signed out of a Cardinal try-out camp in 1953, Tom Cheney played for the St. Louis organization at Albany, Georgia before making the majors in 1957. He was named to the American Association All Star team in 1956 and 1957 while at Omaha.

Cheney was brought up to the Pirates from their Columbus

farm club in July of 1960. He won two of his first three starts - both over the Cincinnati Reds. This included a 5-0 complete game shutout on July 17 where he gave up only four hits.

Working most of the 1960 season as a spot starter and relief man, he finished with a 2-2 record.

RECORDS

YEAR	CLUB	LEAGUE	G	GS	CG	IP	H	BB	SO	W	L	SHO	E.R.A.
1960	Pittsburgh	National	11	8	1	52	44	33	35	2	2	1	3.98

WORLD SERIES

1960	Pittsburgh	National	3	0	0	4	4	1	6	0	0	0	4.50

Joseph O'Neal Christopher - Outfielder #23

Born on December 13, 1935 at Frederiksted, St. Croix, Virgin Islands. Bats and throws right. Height - 5-10. Weight - 176. How obtained - Product of Pittsburgh Farm System.

Joe Christopher was signed by the Pirates in 1955 based upon his performance in the National Baseball Congress Tournament in Wichita, Kansas the previous year.

The best hitter in the Bucs Spring Training in 1960, Joe broke into the majors in 1959 when Roberto Clemente was hurt, but played just five games before he himself was injured. By the time he had recovered, Clemente had too, necessitating Christopher's return to the minors.

Christopher was optioned to Salt Lake City in mid-May, 1960, after starting the season with Pittsburgh, but was recalled after two weeks.

Known as "Hurryin' Joe" due to his speed on the bases, Joe won several early season games for the Pirates with his speed and daring..

RECORDS

YEAR	CLUB	LEAGUE	G	AB	R	H	2B	3B	HR	RBI	AVG.
1960	S. Lake City	P.C.L.	20	82	23	28	5	0	4	10	.341

WORLD SERIES

YEAR	CLUB	LEAGUE	G	AB	R	H	2B	3B	HR	RBI	AVG.
1960	Pittsburgh	National	3	0	2	0	0	0	0	0	.000

Gino Nicholas Cimoli - Outfielder   #20

Born on December 18, 1929, San Francisco, California. Bats and Throws Right. Height -6-2. Weight- 190. How obtained - Trader to Pittsburgh with pitcher Tom Chaney from St. Louis for pitcher Ronnie Kline, December 21, 1959.

Signed originally into the Brooklyn organization by Branch Rickey, Jr., Gino played with four Dodger farm teams before making it to the big leagues in 1956. That year he appeared in his first World Series. Traded to St. Louis for Wally Moon in the winter of 1958, the Pirates obtained him the following year.

Cimoli was a steady performer for the Pirates in 1960. At one time or another he played all three outfield spots. Although over the .300 mark half of the season, he finished with a .267 batting average. His line drive type of hitting was well suited to Forbes Field.

It was Gino, pinch hitting for Roy Face in the 7th game of the World Series, who started the Pirate rally in the eighth inning with a single to right field. He ended up on second when Bill Virdon's grounder took a crazy bounce and struck Yankee Tony Kubek in the throat.

YEAR	CLUB	LEAGUE	G	AB	R	H	2B	3B	HR	RBI	AVG
				RECORDS							
1960	Pittsburgh	National	101	307	36	82	14	4	0	28	.267
				WORLD SERIES							
1960	Pittsburgh	National	7	20	4	5	0	0	0	1	.250

Roberto Walker Clemente - Outfielder #21

Born on August 18, 1934 at Carolina, Puerto Rico. Bats and throws right. Height - 5-11. Weight - 175. How obtained - Drafted from Montreal at Winter Baseball Meetings, November 22, 1954.

Roberto Clemente played his first game four months before his 21st birthday. Signed in Puerto Rico by a Brooklyn scout, Clemente played only one year of minor league ball in 1954 at Montreal. He was drafted by the Pirates that winter.

Clemente was a very consistent hitter in 1960. He hit over .300 all year long, and had only one "slump" where he went hitless in four straight games. His batting average of .314 was fourth highest in the league.

Roberto was named to the National League's All Star team in 1960 and he also led the league's outfielders in assists with 19, and was the only player, Pirate or Yankee, to hit safely in all seven World Series games.

It was Clemente's speed on the bases that kept the Pirate rally alive in the 8th inning of the seventh game of the World Series when he beat out a roller to first base, scoring Bill Virdon from third with the Pirates' sixth run. Hal Smith then hit the home run that put the Pirates ahead.

In 1960 Clemente was given the Most Popular Pirate Award by the fans of Pittsburgh.

YEAR	CLUB	LEAGUE	RECORDS								
			G	AB	R	H	2B	3B	HR	RBI	AVG.
1960	Pittsburgh	National	144	570	89	179	22	6	16	94	.314

YEAR	CLUB	LEAGUE	ALL STAR GAME								
1960	Pittsburgh	National	2	1	0	0	0	0	0	0	.000

YEAR	CLUB	LEAGUE	WORLD SERIES								
1960	Pittsburgh	National	7	29	1	9	0	0	0	3	.310

Bennie Daniels, Jr. - Pitcher #29

Born on June 17, 1932 at Tuscaloosa, Alabama. Bats left. Throws right. Height - 6 11/2. Weight - 190. How obtained - Product of Pittsburgh Farm System.

Bennie Daniels lettered in baseball, basketball, football and track in high school. He played Legion baseball for two years in Compton. Rosey Gilhousen, the Pirates' west coast scout, signed Daniels in 1951. He has played minor league ball at Great Falls, Lincoln, Billings, Hollywood and Columbus. Bennie was brought up to the Pirates for the first time at the end of the 1957 season.

Daniels spent most of the 1958 season in Columbus, and was used mainly for relief in 1959.

Bennie was used sparingly by the Pirates in 1960, getting into only 10 games.

YEAR	CLUB	LEAGUE	RECORDS									
			G	GS	CG	IP	H	BB	SO	W	L	SHO	E.R.A.
1960	Pittsburgh	National	10	6	0	40.1	52	17	16	1	3	0	7.81

ElRoy Leon Face - Pitcher   #26

Born on February 20, 1928 at Stephentown, New York. Bats right and left. Throws right. Height - 5-8. Weight - 155. How obtained - Drafted from Montreal at Winter Baseball Meetings, December 1, 1952.

Originally signed by the Philadelphia Phillies in 1949, Face was drafted in the Brooklyn Dodgers organization in 1951 and then drafted by Pittsburgh in 1952.

Roy's 18-1 record in 1959 gave him the highest winning percentage in a season in major league history - .947. He broke a 49 year old record set in 1910 by Deacon Phillippe for most consecutive wins in a season, and his 18 wins in one year, 17 straight in one year and 22 straight over two seasons, are all major league marks for a relief pitcher. In 1956 he set another major league mark by relieving in 9 consecutive games.

The "Baron of the Bullpen" had another great year in 1960 tying his own Pittsburgh club record for most game appearances when he pitched in his 65th game on the next to the last day of the season.

ElRoy worked in all four of the Pirates' World Series victories, getting credit for three saves. He pitched the last two innings of Game 1 to preserve Vern Law's lead and win. In Game 4 he pitched the last two and two-thirds innings, again preserving the lead and win for Law. The next day in Game 5, he came on in the 7th and again worked in two and two-thirds innings to preserve the lead and win for Harvey Haddix. In the final game, Roy pitched three relief innings and it was Gino Cimoli, his pinch hitter, who started the Pirates' big eighth inning rally.

RECORDS

YEAR	CLUB	LEAGUE	G	GS	CG	IP	H	BB	SO	W	L	SHO	E.R.A.
1960	Pittsburgh	National	68	0	0	115	93	29	72	10	8	0	2.90

ALL STAR GAMES

YEAR	CLUB	LEAGUE	G	GS	CG	IP	H	BB	SO	W	L	SHO	E.R.A.
1960	Pittsburgh	National	1	0	0	1.2	0	0	2	0	0	0	0.00

WORLD SERIES

YEAR	CLUB	LEAGUE	G	GS	CG	IP	H	BB	SO	W	L	SHO	E.R.A.
1960	Pittsburgh	National	4	0	0	10.1	9	2	4	0	0	0	5.16

Earl Coleman Francis - Pitcher #47

Born on July 14, 1936 at Slab Fork, West Virginia. Bats and throws right. Height - 6-2. Weight - 210. How obtained - Product of Pittsburgh farm System.

Earl Francis started out in 1954 with Clinton before spending four year in the United States Air Force. After his return in 1959, he jumped to Salt Lake City.

Earl pitched most of 1960 for Columbus. Bothered part of the season with a sore arm, Francis got into only seven games with the Pirates in the 1960 season.

RECORDS

YEAR	CLUB	LEAGUE	G	GS	CG	IP	H	BB	SO	W	L	SHO	E.R.A.
1960	Pittsburgh	National	7	0	0	18	14	4	8	1	0	0	2.00

Robert Bartmess Friend - Pitcher #19

Born on November 24, 1930, at Lafayette, Indiana. Bats and throws right. Height - 6. Weight - 190. How obtained - Product of Pittsburgh Farm System.

Bob Friend had an outstanding high school and American Legion record in West Lafayette, Indiana. He lettered in baseball, football, basketball and golf in high school, captained the football team and was an All State halfback in 1948. He was All State in baseball in 1949. Bob played four years of American Legion baseball and spent only one season, 1950, in the minors.

The Pirates' player representative came back from a miserable 1959 season to be voted the national League "Comeback of the year" for 1960.

Friend tossed four shutouts in 1960 - two over Cincinnati, one against Philadelphia and the other against St. Louis. Of his 12 losses in 1960, two were by one run margins, five by two runs and one by a three run margin. His record for 1960 could easily have been more impressive. He saved the only game he didn't start, against Milwaukee, on July 5th.

Bob started and won the All Star Game in Kansas City, and made three appearances in the World Series - two as a starter and one in relief. He came within one of tying the Pittsburgh club record for most strikeouts in a game fanning 11 Phillies on April 28th while shutting them out 3-0.

Against the Phillies on September 20th, he broke the then club strikeout record of 176 strikeouts for a season set in 1912 by Claude Hendrix. He finished the year with 183 strikeouts.

When Bob started and won on July 25th against the Cardinals, he pitched the Pirates back into first place and they never left it again in 1960.

YEAR	CLUB	LEAGUE	G	GS	CG	IP	H	BB	SO	W	L	SHO	E.R.A.
					RECORDS								
1960	Pittsburgh	National	38	37	16	276	266	45	183	18	12	4	3.00
					ALL STAR GAMES								
1960	Pittsburgh	National	1	1	0	3	1	1	2	1	0	0	0.00
					WORLD SERIES								
1960	Pittsburgh	National	3	2	0	6	13	3	7	0	2	0	13.50

Joseph Charles Gibbon - Pitcher #22

Born on April 10, 1935, at Hickory, Mississippi. Bats right. Throws left. Height - 6-4.

Weight - 209. How obtained - Product of Pittsburgh Farm System.

As an All American basketball player at the University of Mississippi, Joe was the second highest scorer in the country during the 1956-57 season. Signed at the close of the collegiate baseball season in 1957, he reported to the Pirates' Lincoln farm team in the Class A Western League following his graduation.

Due to his good hitting, Gibbon started out as a first baseman, but started pitching after a jammed thumb hindered his hitting. The first 25 innings he pitched were scoreless, and 10 of his 17 games in 1957 were complete games.

Gibbon wasn't even on the Pirates 1960 Spring Training Roster but he showed enough in training as a member of the Columbus club to make the big league.

Joe lost his first big league start in San Francisco in May 8, but came back with strong relief work and made eight other starts during the season.

RECORDS

YEAR	CLUB	LEAGUE	G	GS	CG	IP	H	BB	SO	W	L	SHO	E.R.A.
1960	Pittsburgh	National	27	9	0	80	87	51	60	4	2	0	4.05

WORLD SERIES

YEAR	CLUB	LEAGUE	G	GS	CG	IP	H	BB	SO	W	L	SHO	E.R.A.
1960	Pittsburgh	National	2	0	0	3	4	1	2	0	0	0	9.00

Paul Robert Giel - Pitcher #50

Born on August 29, 1932 at Winons, Minnesota. Bats and throws right. Height - 5-10. Weight - 180. How obtained - Claimed on waivers from San Francisco Giants, April 13, 1959.

An All-American quarterback at the University of Minnesota, Paul Giel signed a bonus contract with the New York Giants in 1954. He entered the Army in November of 1955, and served in Germany for a year and a half. The 1958 season was split between the giants and their Phoenix farm team.

The Pirates claimed Giel on waivers from the Giants in April of 1959. Paul appeared briefly for the Pirates before being sent to Columbus. Giel was a member of the Pirate bullpen briefly in 1960, appearing in 16 games.

RECORDS

YEAR	CLUB	LEAGUE	G	GS	CG	IP	H	BB	SO	W	L	SHO	E.R.A.
1960	Pittsburgh	National	16	0	0	33	35	15	21	2	0	0	5.73

Fred Allen Green - Pitcher #35

Born on September 14, 1933 at Titusville, New Jersey. Bats right. Throws left. Height - 6-4. Weight - 190. How obtained - Product of Pittsburgh Farm System.

Fred Green was signed by the Pirates in 1951 following a workout at Forbes Field. The next year he won 20 games with Brunswick, Georgia in the Georgia-Florida League. Before making the Pirates in 1959, he played for Waco, Williamsport, New Orleans, Williamsport, New Orleans, Hollywood, Salt lake City and Columbus.

Green was second only to Roy Face in relief appearances in 1960, appearing in 45 games with an 8-4 record and a 3.21 E.R.A. He was also credited with eight saves. Fred made five straight relief appearances in July, pitching 10 innings without giving up a run. In 70 innings of pitching he gave up only four homeruns and hit two himself.

YEAR	CLUB	LEAGUE	G	GS	CG	IP	H	BB	SO	W	L	SHO	E.R.A.
					RECORDS								
1960	Pittsburgh	National	45	0	0	70	61	33	49	8	4	0	3.21
					WORLD SERIES								
1960	Pittsburgh	National	3	0		4	11	1	3	0	0	0	22.50

Richard Morrow Groat - Shortstop #24

Born on November 4, 1930 at Swissvale, Pa. Bats and throws right. Height - 6.

Weight - 180. Bats and throws right. How obtained - Signed by Pirates following graduation from Duke.

Dick Groat is one of the few major league players to step off a college campus into major league baseball without an inning of minor league experience. An All American in baseball and basketball at Duke University, he played his first major league game three days after he graduated.

Groat, the Pirates' team captain, won the 1960 batting championship on the last day of the season in a battle with Norm Larker of the Dodgers, .325 to .323. His outstanding clutch hitting, defensive play and teamwork were recognized when he was voted the League's Most Valuable Player. He was the first Pirate to receive the MVP award since Arky Vaughn in 1935, and the first Pirates to lead the League in hitting since Debs Garms in 1940.

Dick was named to the League's All Star team for the second straight year in 1960. On July 17th, he got his 1,000th major league hit. He was over the .300 mark all but five days, and was hitting .325 when Lew Burdette of the Braves hit him on the left wrist in the first inning on September 6th at Forbes Field. Not wanting to win the batting title by default, and anxious to play in his first World Series, he ran and stayed in shape until his cast was removed. He returned to action as a pinch runner on September 27th, as a pinch hitter on the 30th, and took over his shortstop position for the final two games of the season, finishing with a .325 average and the batting title.

RECORDS

YEAR	CLUB	LEAGUE	G	AB	R	H	2B	3B	HR	RBI	AVG.
1960	Pittsburgh	National	138	573	85	186	26	4	2	50	.325

ALL STAR GAMES

1960	Pittsburgh	National	2	2	0	0	0	0	0	0	.000

WORLD SERIES

1960	Pittsburgh	National	7	28	3	6	2	0	0	2	.214

Donald John Gross - Pitcher #38

Born on June 30, 1931 at Weidman, Michigan. Bats and throws left. Height - 5-11. Weight - 184. How obtained - Traded to Pittsburgh from Cincinnati in exchange for pitcher Bob Purkey, December 9, 1957.

When Don Gross was seven years old, he caught his right arm

in a washing machine wringer. While recuperating, he began to pitch lefthanded. Don was a baseball, basketball and track star at Weidman High School in Michigan, and attended Michigan State University for one year on a basketball scholarship.

Gross signed with Cincinnati and played with the Reds in 1957 prior to being traded to the Pirates.

In 1958 he appeared in 40 games in relief and had 12 saves. Bothered by a sore arm in 1959, he still pitched in 21 games.

Injured for most of the 1960 season, Don appeared in only five games.

RECORDS

YEAR	CLUB	LEAGUE	G	GS	CG	IP	H	BB	SO	W	L	SHO	E.R.A.
1960	Pittsburgh	National	5	0	0	5.1	5	0	3	0	0	0	3.38

Harvey Haddix, Jr. - Pitcher #31

Born on September 18, 1925 at Medway, Ohio. Bats and throws left. Height - 5-9.

Weight - 160. How obtained - Traded to Pirates with Smoky Burgess and Don Hoak from Cincinnati, January 31, 1959, for Frank Thomas, Whammy Douglas, Jim Pendleton and Johnny Powers.

Harvey Haddix broke into organized baseball in 1947 with Winston Salem, pitched for the next three years for Columbus, then entered the service. Discharged in 1952, he joined the Cardinals, where he stayed until traded to Cincinnati in 1957. In 1959, he joined the Pirates and experienced one of baseball's most memorable moments.

On Tuesday night, May 26, 1959, at Milwaukee's County Stadium, Haddix pitched the first nine-inning perfect game in National League history, the first extra-inning perfect game in major league history, and the longest string of perfect innings ever put together in a major league game. Unfortunately, he lost his perfect game, his no-hitter and the game in the 13th, 1-0, on an error, an intentional walk and a hit.

Haddix earned two of the Pirates four wins in the World Series - one as a starter and one in relief. He started the 5th game of the Series in Yankee Stadium, going 6 and 1/3 innings. With a 4-2 lead, he had given up only 5 hits and struck out 6. Roy Face came on in the 7th to protect the win.

In the 7th game, he came on in the top of the 9th with two men on, retired Maris on a pop foul, but gave up a single to Mantle which scored a run. Yogi Berra then ground out, scoring another run. Finally he retired Skowron on a force out. He was the pitcher of record when Mazeroski hit his game-winning home run in the bottom of the 9th.

RECORDS

YEAR	CLUB	LEAGUE	G	GS	CG	IP	H	BB	SO	W	L	SHO	E.R.A.
1960	Pittsburgh	National	29	28	4	172	189	38	101	11	10	0	3.98

WORLD SERIES

YEAR	CLUB	LEAGUE	G	GS	CG	IP	H	BB	SO	W	L	SHO	E.R.A.
1960	Pittsburgh	National	2	1	0	7.1	6	2	6	2	0	0	2.46

Donald Albert Hoak - Third Baseman   #12

Born on February 5, 1928, at Roulette, Pennsylvania. Bats and throws right.

Height - 6-1/2. Weight - 175. How obtained - Traded to Pittsburgh with Harvey Haddix and Smoky Burgess from Cincinnati for Frank Thomas, Whammy Douglas, Jim Pendelton and Johnny Powers on January 31, 1959.

Don Hoak left high school during World War II to enlist in the Marines, seeing action in the South Pacific. He did some boxing in the Corps at Paris Island, and when he was discharged, he turned pro as a welterweight with 27 victories in 39 fights with

18 knock-outs. After finishing high school Don turned to pro baseball, signing with the Dodgers in 1947. Don was part of the Brooklyn championship team in 1955 before being traded to the Cubs and then Cincinnati.

After coming to the Pirates in 1959, Don had the club's longest hitting streak - in 14 games - From June 4th through the 16th, when he collected 24 hits in 54 at bats for a .444 average.

Nicknamed "Tiger" by play-by-play announcer Bob Prince, Hoak played with pulled muscles, groin injuries, and a severe cut on his foot. Don got off to a slow start in '60, hitting only .260 at the All Star game, but through the last half of the year he hit .301.

The driving force behind the Pirates spectacular 1960 season, his watch-words of: "We'll play 'em one at a time," and "You gotta keep drivin'," became team slogans.

YEAR	CLUB	LEAGUE	RECORDS								
			G	AB	R	H	2B	3B	HR	RBI	AVG.
1960	Pittsburgh	National	155	553	97	156	24	9	16	79	.282
			WORLD SERIES								
1960	Pittsburgh	National	7	23	3	5	2	0	0	3	.217

Daniel Kravitz - Catcher #10

Born on December 21, 1930 at Lopez, Pennsylvania. Bats left. Throws right. Height - 6. Weight - 200. How obtained - Product of Pittsburgh Farm System.

Danny Kravitz played for Pittsburgh minor league teams at Greenville, Mayfield, Charleston and Waco prior to going into the Marines in 1952. Originally an outfielder, Danny switched to catching while in the Marines.

Returning in 1954, Kravitz played for New Orleans,

Hollywood and Columbus before joining the Pirates in 1958 and 1959.

Kravitz opened the 1960 season with the Pirates, but only played eight games before being sold to the Kansas City Athletics on May 31.

			RECORDS							
YEAR	CLUB	LEAGUE	G	AB	R	H	2B	3B	HR	RBI	AVG.
1960	Pittsburgh	National	8	6	0	0	0	0	0	0	.000

Clement Walker Labine - Pitcher   #29

Born on August 6, 1926, at Lincoln, Rhode Island. Bats and throws right. Height - 6 ½.

Weight - 195. How obtained - Signed by Pittsburgh as a free agent, August 16, 1960.

Clem Labine broke into pro ball with the Dodgers' farm team at Newport News in 1944, and made the parent club in 1950. For eight years, he was the Dodgers' best relief man. Clem played in four World Series with the Dodgers.

Labine came to the Pirates late in 1960. Los Angeles cut him lose on June 15, and he signed with the Detroit Tigers. Former Pirate, Hank Foiles, then with Detroit, saw a release coming for Labine and contacted the Pirates. Pirate scout George Detore looked Labine over, and Clem was signed by General Manager Joe L. Brown.

Clem signed with the Pirates on August 16, and saw action the very next night. He struck out six Phillies in three innings of relief. Used mainly as a short relief man, Clem appeared in 15 games, worked 30 innings, won three, lost none, saved four games and had a 1.49 E.R.A. In the first three weeks he was with the Pirates he won two, saved four and allowed only three runs in 15 innings.

RECORDS

YEAR	CLUB	LEAGUE	G	GS	CG	IP	H	BB	SO	W	L	SHO	E.R.A.
1960	L.A./Pgh.	National	28	0	0	47	55	19	36	3	1	0	3.06
1960	Detroiot	American	14	0	0	19	19	12	6	0	3	0	5.20

WORLD SERIES

1960	Pittsburgh	National	3	0	0	4	13	1	2	0	0	0	13.50

Vernon Sanders Law - Pitcher   **#32**

Born on March 12, 1930, at Meridian, Idaho. Bats and throws right. Height - 6-3. Weight 195. How obtained - Product of the Pittsburgh Farm System.

Vern, a product of the Pittsburgh Farm System, was signed through the efforts of Bing Crosby and U.S. Senator Herman Walker of Idaho. He played for Pirate farm teams at Santa Rosa, Davenport and New Orleans before making the parent club in 1951.

Law won his first four starts in 1960, all complete games, and later in the season won eight straight. The Pirates' longest losing streaks in 1960 were four-gamers - twice - and on both occasions, it was Law who stopped them. Both times were against the Los Angeles Dodgers and Johnny Podres at the Coliseum in Los Angeles. The first losing streak halted was May 10 with a 3-2 win, and the other was a 10-2 win on August 20. Both were complete games.

Law, known as "The Deacon" because of his ordination as a Mormon minister, beat the Dodgers and Cardinals five times each in 1960 and had victories over every other club in the nation League but Milwaukee. He appeared in relief in the 1st All Star Game in Kansas City and started and received credit for the win in the 2nd game in New York.

Vern pitched three shutouts in 1960 and tied Lew Burdette

and Warren Spahn of Milwaukee with 18 complete games. Even though he won 20 games, Law's record could have been better. Four of his nine losses were by one run, one by two runs and another by three.

Law pitched the last few weeks of the season and the World Series with a badly sprained ankle. With the help of Roy Face he started and won games one and four in the Series. He started game seven, going five innings before being taken out due to the strain on his ankle.

Vernon Law capped his 1960 season by earning the Cy Young Award as the best pitcher in the Major Leagues.

						RECORDS							
YEAR	CLUB	LEAGUE	G	GS	CG	IP	H	BB	SO	W	L	SHO	E.R.A.
1960	Pittsburgh	National	35	35	18	272	266	40	120	20	9	3	3.08
						ALL STAR GAME							
1960	Pittsburgh	National	2	1	0	2.2	1	0	1	1	0	0	0.00
						WORLD SERIES							
1960	Pittsburgh	National	3	3	0	18.1	22	3	8	2	0	0	3.44

William Stanley Mazeroski - Second Baseman   #9

Born on September 5, 1936 at Wheeling, West Virginia. Bats and throws right. Height - 5-11. Weight - 182. How obtained - Product of Pittsburgh Farm System.

Bill Mazeroski was an outstanding baseball and basketball player in high school. Following his graduation in 1954, he was signed by the Pirates and played for Williamsport in the Eastern League. Bill spent only one full season in the minors and never played below Class A ball.

In 1955 Maz split the season between Hollywood and Williamsport, and in 1956 he started the season with Hollywood, but joined the Pirates in July.

Bill came back from a poor 1959 season, raising his batting average 32 points to .273, and led the League's second basemen in putouts (413), assists (447), total chances accepted (572) and double plays (127). He made the All Star team in 1958, 1959 and 1960.

The New York Chapter of the Baseball Writers of America presented their annual Babe Ruth Award to Bill as outstanding player in the 1960 World Series.

YEAR	CLUB	LEAGUE	RECORDS								
			G	AB	R	H	2B	3B	HR	RBI	AVG.
1960	Pittsburgh	National	151	538	58	147	21	5	11	64	.273
			ALL STAR GAME								
1960	Pittsburgh	National	2	4	0	1	0	0	0	1	.250
			WORLD SERIES								
1960	Pittsburgh	National	7	25	4	8	2	0	2	5	.320

Roman Gomez Mejias - Outfielder #15

Born on August 9, 1932 at Las Villas, Cuba. Bats and throws right. Height - 6. Weight - 175. How obtained - Product of Pittsburgh Farm System.

Signed out of a Pittsburgh tryout camp in Cuba in 1953, Roman Mejias had previously only played high school baseball. His first year at Class D Batavia, he led the league in stolen bases with 42. With Waco in 1954, he set a record by hitting in 54 straight games.

Roman made the Pirates in 1955, went back to the minors with Hollywood in 1956, then returned to Pittsburgh in 1957. He was the Pirates' reserve outfielder in 1958 and 1959.

Mejias played only three games in the 1960 season with the pirates before being farmed to Columbus. He was recalled near the end of the season, but broke his wrist in a game the weekend before he was to arrive.

			RECORDS								
YEAR	CLUB	LEAGUE	G	AB	R	H	2B	3B	HR	RBI	AVG.
1960	Pittsburgh	National	3	1	1	0	0	0	0	0	.000

Wilmer David (Vinegar Bend) Mizell - Pitcher   #30

Born on August 13, 1930 at Vinegar Bend, Alabama. Bats right. Throws left. Height - 6-3. Weight - 205. How obtained - Traded to Pittsburgh along with outfielder Dick Gray from St. Louis Cardinals for infielder Julian Javier and pitcher Ed Bauta, May 28, 1960.

Mizell signed with St. Louis following his graduation from Leaksville, Mississippi High School. Before making the Cardinals in 1952, he played for their farm teams at Albany, Winston-Salem and Houston.

Coming to the Pirates in a deal with the Cardinals, Mizell came from St. Louis with a 1-3 record. He became the fourth starter giving left-hand balance to the staff of Law, Friend and Haddix.

"Vinegar Bend" pitched three shutouts for the Pirates. In Chicago on July 29, he gave up only two singles to win 4-0. Then he scattered four singles and a double to shut out the Giants 1-0. Finally, on September 18, he beat the Cincinnati Reds at Crosley Field 1-0 on three singles.

At one stretch in 1960, from the second inning July 22 at San Francisco through two shutouts (July 29 and August 5), and through four innings of the August 4th game, Mizell pitched 30 scoreless innings.

Mizell did not see Mazeroski's Series winning home run. Haddix, the pitcher, was due up after Maz and was to be hit for by Dick Stuart. Mizell had been warming up in the bullpen preparing to enter the game in the 10th inning. He was walking under the stands on his way to the dugout when the homer was hit.

						RECORDS							
YEAR	CLUB	LEAGUE	G	GS	CG	IP	H	BB	SO	W	L	SHO	E.R.A.
1960	St. L./Pitt.	National	32	32	8	211	205	74	113	14	8	3	3.50

						WORLD SERIES							
1960	Pittsburgh	National	2	1	0	2.1	4	2	1	0	1	0	15.43

Glenn Richard Nelson - First baseman   #14

Born on November 18, 1924, at Portsmouth, Ohio. Bats and throws left. Height - 5-11. Weight - 191. How obtained - Drafted by Pittsburgh from Toronto at Winter baseball Meetings, December 1, 1958.

In pro baseball since 1942, Rocky Nelson for years was a star with Montreal and Toronto in the International League. Leading the AAA many times in home runs and RBIs, Rocky w on the League's Most Valuable Player Award in 1953, 1955 and 1958. Nelson played briefly for the Pirates, Cardinals, White Sox, Dodgers and Indians before the Pirates drafted him in 1959. That year he hit .291 and was the team's most dependable pinch hitter.

Rocky started the first and seventh games of the 1960 World Series. It was his two-run home run in the first inning of game seven that gave the Pirates an early lead.

| | | | RECORDS | | | | | | | |
YEAR	CLUB	LEAGUE	G	AB	R	H	2B	3B	HR	RBI	AVG.
1960	Pittsburgh	National	93	200	34	60	11	1	7	35	.300

			WORLD SERIES							
1960	Pittsburgh	National	4	9	2	3	0	0	1	2	.333

Robert Carl Oldis - Catcher #2

Born on January 5, 1929 at Preston, Iowa. Bats and throws right. Height - 6-1. Weight - 190. How obtained - Drafted from Denver at Winter Baseball Meetings, November 30, 1959.

Bob Oldis got into baseball by paying his own way to the Jack Rossiter Baseball School in Cocoa, Florida and was signed out of the school in 1949 by the Washington Senators. He made the parent club in 1953 after time in Emporia, Charlotte and Chatanooga. He also played in Denver and Richmond, New York Yankee farm clubs, before being drafted by Pittsburgh.

Although appearing in only 22 regular season games and briefly in 2 Series games, Bob was always at the ball park early pitching batting practice for anyone who wanted extra work or catching pitchers who wanted to throw.

Oldis typified the hustle, drive and spirit of the 1960 Pittsburgh Pirates.

| | | | RECORDS | | | | | | | |
YEAR	CLUB	LEAGUE	G	AB	R	H	2B	3B	HR	RBI	AVG.
1960	Pittsburgh	National	22	20	1	4	1	1	0	1	.200

			WORLD SERIES							
1960	Pittsburgh	National	2	0	0	0	0	0	0	0	.000

Diomedes Antonio Olivo - Pitcher #17

Born on January 20, 1920 at Guayubin, Dominican Republic. Bats and throws left. Height - 6-1. Weight - 195. How obtained - Purchased from Poza Rica, Mexico of the Mexican League in March, 1960.

An outstanding hitter in the minor leagues, Diomedes Olivo was often used as a pinch-hitter or in the outfield when he wasn't pitching. With the Mexico City Reds of the Mexican League, he hit .359 in 1956 and .351 in 1958.

Olivo came up to the Pirates late in the 1960 season, getting into only four games.

RECORDS

YEAR	CLUB	LEAGUE	G	GS	CG	IP	H	BB	SO	W	L	SHO	E.R.A.
1960	Pittsburgh	National	4	0	0	9.2	8	5	10	0	0	0	2.79

John Richard Schofield - Infielder #11

Born on January 7, 1935 at Springfield, Illinois. Bats right and left. Throws right.

Height - 5-9. Weight - 165. How obtained - Traded to Pittsburgh by St. Louis for infielders Gene Freese and Johnny O'Brien, June 15, 1958.

Dick Schofield inherited the nickname Ducky and a professional baseball career from his father. His father never made the majors, but Dick signed with the St. Louis Cardinals after his high school graduation as a bonus player. After some minor league experience with Omaha, he spent two years with the Cardinals before being traded to Pittsburgh.

Until the night of September 6, 1960, Dick had seen action in only 44 games. But on that night he came into the game when Dick Groat was struck by a pitch from Milwaukee's Lew

Burdette. That night Dick got three hits and made a play deep in the shortstop hole to help pull rookie Joe Gibbon out of a jam.

When it was announced that Dick Groat's wrist had been broken, Schofield had to play shortstop indefinitely.

In the 19 games in which he subbed for Groat, he hit for a .368 average with four doubles, a triple and seven RBIs. He hit .333 for the season and .33 as a pinch hitter in the World Series.

RECORDS

YEAR	CLUB	LEAGUE	G	AB	R	H	2B	3B	HR	RBI	AVG.
1960	Pittsburgh	National	65	102	9	34	4	1	0	10	.333

WORLD SERIES

YEAR	CLUB	LEAGUE	G	AB	R	H	2B	3B	HR	RBI	AVG.
1960	Pittsburgh	National	3	3	0	1	0	0	0	0	.333

Robert Ralph Skinner - Outfielder   #4

Born on October 3, 1931, at LaJolla, California. Bats left. Throws right. Height - 6-4. Weight - 185. How obtained - Product of Pittsburgh Farm System.

A onetime first baseman in the minors, Bob Skinner played that position most of the season for the pirates in 1954. With New Orleans in 1955, he led the league in batting with a .346 average until he broke his wrist. Back with the Pirates in 1956, Skinner became the regular left fielder when manager Bobby Bragan moved Frank Thomas from left field to third base.

Skinner started off the 1960 season by hitting safely in his first nine games. He had an 11 game hitting streak, two nine game streaks, four eight gamers, two seven gamers and one six game. His longest batting slumps of the year were of three games - once in June and again in August.

Bob was also the National League's left fielder in the two 1960 All Star games.

Jamming his thumb in the first game of the 1960 World Series,

Skinner sat out the next five games, returning for game seven.

In the seventh game, it was Skinner who laid down a perfect bunt to advance Bill Virdon and Dick Groat in the crucial eighth inning.

YEAR	CLUB	LEAGUE	G	AB	R	H	2B	3B	HR	RBI	AVG.
			RECORDS								
1960	Pittsburgh	National	145	571	83	156	33	6	15	86	.273
			ALL STAR GAME								
1960	Pittsburgh	National	2	7	1	2	0	0	0	1	.286
			WORLD SERIES								
1960	Pittsburgh	National	2	5	2	1	0	0	0	1	.200

Harold Wayne Smith - Catcher #5

Born on December 7, 1930 at West Frankfort, Illinois. Bats and throws right. Height - 6. Weight 195. How obtained - Traded to Pittsburgh from Kansas City in exchange for pitcher Dick Hall and infielder Ken Hamlin, December 15, 1959.

Hal Smith was originally signed into the New York Yankees organization and played for Ventura, Newark, Quincy, Beaumont, Birmingham and Columbus. At Columbus in 1954, Hal led the American Association with a .350 batting average. He was then traded to Baltimore in 1955, as part of a 17 player trade. In 1956 he was part of a six player trade between Baltimore and Kansas City, Finally, he came to Pittsburgh during the 1959 inter-league trading period..

In addition to catching, Smith plays first and third base.

In the off season Hal Smith and ElRoy Face played guitars and sang in supper clubs, at banquets and on radio and TV.

			RECORDS								
YEAR	CLUB	LEAGUE	G	AB	R	H	2B	3B	HR	RBI	AVG.
1960	Pittsburgh	National	77	258	37	76	18	2	11	45	.295
			WORLD SERIES								
1960	Pittsburgh	National	3	8	1	3	0	0	1	3	.375

R. C. Stevens - First baseman   #7

Born on July 22, 1934 at Moultrie, Georgia. Bats right. Throws left. Height - 6-4 1/2. Weight - 208. How obtained - Product of Pittsburgh Farm System.

R. C. Stevens was taken to the Pirates' minor league tryout camp in 1952 by his high school baseball coach. He was signed and spent time at Batavia, St. Jean, Burlington, Hollywood, Columbus and Salt Lake.

R. C. started the 1058 season with the Pirates, and then in 1959, spent six months in the Army Reserve before joining them in late May.

Stevens spent most of the 1960 season in the minors, appearing in only nine games for the Pirates, usually as a late inning defensive replacement.

			RECORDS								
YEAR	CLUB	LEAGUE	G	AB	R	H	2B	3B	HR	RBI	AVG.
1960	Pittsburgh	National	9	3	1	0	0	0	0	0	.000

Richard Lee Stuart - First baseman   #7

Born on November 7, 1932, at San Francisco, California. Bats and throws right.

Height - 6-3 Weight - 210. How obtained - Product of Pittsburgh Farm System.

Dick Stuart had exhibited his home run power from the time he broke into pro ball in 1951. He led the Pioneer League in home runs twice and hit a record 66 home runs with Lincoln in the Western League, becoming one of nine minor league players to hit 60 or more home runs in one season.

Coming up to the Pirates in mid-season 1958, Stuart was largely responsible for helping the team to its second place finish. He hit some of the longest home runs ever hit in Chicago's Wrigley Field and Pittsburgh's Forbes Field.

Stuart started slowly in 1960, but gained momentum during the latter part of the season. His biggest day came on June 30 in the second game of a twi-night doubleheader with San Francisco at Forbes Field. In that game he hit three consecutive home runs, The first was hit in the first inning with two men on off Mike McCormick, the second in the third inning against Billy Loes, and another in the fifth off Stu Miller. In the other two at bats he singled and grounded out. He ended the night with seven RBIs.

RECORDS

YEAR	CLUB	LEAGUE	G	AB	R	H	2B	3B	HR	RBI	AVG.
1960	Pittsburgh	National	122	438	48	114	17	5	23	83	.260

WORLD SERIES

1960	Pittsburgh	National	5	20	0	3	0	0	0	0	.150

James Umbricht - Pitcher #37

Born on September 17, 1930 at Chicago, Illinois. Bats and throws right. Height - 6-4. Weight - 215. How obtained - Traded by Milwaukee farm system to Pittsburgh for outfielder Emil Panko, April 6, 1959.

Jim Umbricht signed into the Milwaukee Braves organization in 1953, following his graduation from the University of Georgia. Jim spent a year in the minors, then two years in the

Army. He played with Braves' farm teams at Waycross, Baton Rouge, Topeka and Atlanta before his trade to Pittsburgh.

After starting the 1960 season with the Pirates and seeing action in 17 games, Jim was farmed to Columbus in mid-season.

YEAR	CLUB	LEAGUE	G	GS	CG	IP	H	BB	SO	W	L	SHO	E.R.A.
1960	Pittsburgh	National	17	3	0	40.2	40	27	26	1	2	0	5.09

William Charles Virdon - Outfielder #18

Born on June 9, 1931 at Hazel Park, Michigan. Bats left. Throws right. Height - 6. Weight - 180. How obtained - Traded to Pittsburgh by St. Louis in exchange for outfielder Bobby DelGreco and pitcher Dick Littlefield on May 16, 1956.

Bill Virdon was was playing Ban Johnson Baseball in Kansas when he was scouted and signed by the new York Yankee organization in 1950. He played for Independence, Kansas City, Norfolk, Binghampton, and Birmingham in the Yankee system before going to the Cardinals in 1954 as part of the Enos Slaughter trade. Virdon won the International League batting championship with St. Louis' Rochester team in 1955 with a .333 average, and went to the majors in 1955. He was the '55 National League Rookie of the Year with St. Louis. In 1956 he was the National League's second hitter as he split the season with St. Louis and Pittsburgh.

Virdon played a very important role in the 1960 World Series with both his timely hitting and his spectacular catches.

YEAR	CLUB	LEAGUE	G	AB	R	H	2B	3B	HR	RBI	AVG.
1960	Pittsburgh	National	120	409	60	108	16	9	8	40	.264
WORLD SERIES											
1960	Pittsburgh	National	7	29	2	7	3	0	0	5	.241

George Adrian Witt - Pitcher #39

Born on November 9, 1933, at Long Beach, California. Bats and throws right.

Height - 6-3. Weight -200. How obtained - Drafted from Pueblo at Winter Baseball Meetings, November 30, 1954.

Signed originally by the Brooklyn Dodgers in 1950, George Witt played with the Greenwood and Three Rivers farm teams. Before coming to the Pittsburgh organization in 1954, he spent two years in the Marines.

In 1958 Witt had an outstanding rookie year with the Pirates winning nine and losing two with a 1.61 ERA.

A sore elbow developed in spring training in 1959 which limited him to 15 games. In 1960 he started the season with the Pirates, but after three games he was farmed to Salt Lake City. He was 7-3 there and rejoined the Pirates in July, winning his first game on August 4, 4-1 against the Dodgers.

RECORDS

YEAR	CLUB	LEAGUE	G	GS	CG	IP	H	BB	SO	W	L	SHO	E.R.A.
1960	S. L. City	P.C.L.	12	12	5	73	62	43	55	7	3	2	4.32
1960	Pittsburgh	National	10	6	0	30	33	12	15	1	2	0	4.20

WORLD SERIES

YEAR	CLUB	LEAGUE	G	GS	CG	IP	H	BB	SO	W	L	SHO	E.R.A.
1960	Pittsburgh	National	3	0	0	2.2	5	2	1	0	0	0	0.00

APPENDIX B
1960 League Leaders

1960 National and American League Batting Leaders

BATTING AVERAGE:

Dick Groat	Pittsburgh	.325	Pete Runnels	Boston	.320
Norm Larker	Los Angeles	.323	Al Smith	Chicago	.315
Willie Mays	San Francisco	.319	Minnie Minoso	Chicago	.311
Roberto Clemente	Pittsburgh	.314	Bill Skowron	New York	.309
Ken Boyer	St. Louis	.304	Harvey Kuenn	Cleveland	.308

HITS

Willie Mays	San Francisco	190	Minnie Minoso	Chicago	184
Vada Pinson	Cincinnati	187	Brooks Robinson	Baltimore	175
Dick Groat	Pittsburgh	186	Nellie Fox	Chicago	175
Bill Bruton	Milwaukee	180	Al Smith	Chicago	169
			Pete Runnels	Boston	169

DOUBLES

Vada Pinson	Cincinnati	37	Tito Francona	Cleveland	36
Orlando Cepeda	San Francisco	36	Bill Skowron	New York	34
Bob Skinner	Pittsburgh	33	Minnie Monoso	Chicago	32
Frank Robinson	Cincinnati	33	Gene Freese	Chicago	32
Ernie Banks	Chicago	32	3 tied with 31		

BEAT 'EM BUCS

TRIPLES

Bill Bruton	Milwaukee	13		Nellie Fox	Chicago	10
Vada Pinson	Cincinnati	12		Brooks Robinson	Baltimore	9
Willie Mays	San Francisco	12		5 tied with 7		
Hank Aaron	Milwaukee	11				
3 tied with 10						

HOME RUNS

Ernie Banks	Chicago	41		Mickey Mantle	New York	40
Hank Aaron	Milwaukee	40		Roger Maris	New York	39
Eddie Mathews	Milwaukee	39		Jim Lemon	Washington	38
Ken Boyer	St. Louis	32		Rocky Colavito	Detroit	35
Frank Robinson	Cincinnati	31		Harmon Killebrew	Washington	31

TOTAL BASES

Hank Aaron	Milwaukee	334		Mickey Mantle	New York	294
Ernie Banks	Chicago	331		Roger Maris	New York	290
Willie Mays	San Francisco	330		Bill Skowron	New York	284
Ken Boyer	St. Louis	310		Minnie Minoso	Chicago	284
Vada Pinson	Cincinnat	308		Bob Lemon	Washington	268

RUNS BATTED IN

Hank Aaron	Milwaukee	126		Roger Maris	New York	112
Eddie Mathews	Milwaukee	124		Minnie Minoso	Chicago	105
Ernie Banks	Chicago	117		Vic Wertz	Boston	103
Willie Mays	San Francisco	103		Bob Lemon	Washington	100
Ken Boyer	St. Louis	97		Jim Gentile	Baltimore	98

RUNS

Bill Bruton	Milwaukee	112		Mickey Mantle	New York	119
Eddie Mathews	Milwaukee	108		Roger Maris	New York	98
Vada Pinson	Cincinnati	107		Minnie Minoso	Chicago	89
Willie Mays	San Francisco	107		Jim Landis	Chicago	89
Hank Aaron	Milwaukee	102		Roy Sievers	Washington	87

BASES ON BALLS

Richie Ashburn	Chicago	116	Eddie Yost	Detroit	125
Eddie Mathews	Milwaukee	111	Mickey Mantle	New York	111
Jim Gilliam	Los Angeles	96	Bob Allison	Washington	92
Frank Robinson	Cincinnati	82	Gene Woodling	Baltimore	84
Daryl Spencer	St. Louis	81	Jim Landis	Chicago	80

STOLEN BASES

Maury Wills	Los Angeles	50	Luis Aparicio	Chicago	51
Vada Pinson	Cincinnati	32	Jim Landis	Chicago	23
Tony Taylor	Chicago/Phil.	26	Lenny Green	Washington	21
Willie Mays	San Francisco	25	Al Kaline	Detroit	19
Bill Bruton	Milwaukee	22	Jim Piersall	Cleveland	18

1960 National and American League Pitching Records

WINNING PERCENTAGE

Ernie Broglio	St. Louis	.700	Jim Perry	Cleveland	.643
Vernon Law	Pittsburgh	.690	Art Ditmar	New York	.625
Warren Spahn	Milwaukee	.677	Chuck Estrada	Baltimore	.621
Bob Buhl	Milwaukee	.640	Milt Pappas	Baltimore	.577
Bob Purkey	Cincinnati	.607	Buddy Daley	Kansas City	.500
			Frank Lary	Detroit	.500

EARNED RUN AVERAGE

Mike McCormick	San Francisco	2.70	Frank Baumann	Chicago	2.67
Ernie Broglio	St. Louis	2.74	Jim Bunning	Detroit	2.79
Don Drysdale	Los Angeles	2.84	Hal Brown	Baltimore	3.06
Stan Williams	Los Angeles	3.00	Art Ditmar	New York	3.06
Bob Friend	Pittsburgh	3.00	Whitey Ford	New York	3.08

WINS

Ernie Broglio	St. Louis	21	Chuck Estrada	Baltimore	18
Warren Spahn	Milwaukee	21	Jim Perry	Cleveland	18
Vernon Law	Pittsburgh	20	Buddy Daley	Kansas City	16
Lew Burdette	Milwaukee	19	Art Ditmar	New York	15
Frank Lary	Detroit	15	Milt Pappas	Baltimore	15

BEAT 'EM BUCS

SAVES

Lindy McDaniel	St. Louis	26		Mike Fornieles	Boston	14
ElRoy Face	Pittsburgh	24		Johnny Klippstein	Cleveland	14
Bill Henry	Cincinnati	17		Ray Moore	Chic./Was.	13
Jim Brosnan	Cincinnati	12		Bobby Shantz	New York	11

STRIKEOUTS

Don Drysdale	Los Angeles	246		Jim Bunning	Detroit	201
Sandy Koufax	Los Angeles	197		Pedro Ramos	Washington	160
Sam Jones	San Francisco	190		Early Wynn	Chicago	158
Ernie Broglio	St. Louis	188		Frank Lary	Detroit	149
Bob Friend	Pittsburgh	183		Chuck Estrada	Baltimore	144

COMPLETE GAMES

Warren Spahn	Milwaukee	21		Camilo Pascual	Washington	17
Lew Burdette	Milwaukee	20		Don Mossi	Detroit	15
Vernon Law	Pittsburgh	20		Milt Pappas	Baltimore	15
Robin Roberts	Philadelphia	19		Jim Bunning	Detroit	14
Johnny Antonelli	San Francisco	17		Early Wynn	Chicago	14
Don Newcombe	Cincinnati	17				

INNINGS PITCHED

Warren Spahn	Milwaukee	292		Early Wynn	Chicago	256
Lew Burdette	Milwaukee	290		Jim Bunning	Detroit	250
Johnny Antoonelli	San Francisco	282		Paul Foytack	Detroit	240

BIBLIOGRAPHY

"The Pittsburgh Press" April-November, 1960

"The Pittsburgh Post Gazette" April – November, 1960

"The New York Times" April – October, 1960

"The Sporting News" October, 1960

"Maz and the '60 Bucs" Jim O'Brien 1993

"The Best Game Ever" Jim Reisler 2007

"1960 Pittsburgh Pirates Yearbook"

"1961 Pittsburgh Pirates Yearbook"

"1960 New York Yankee Yearbook"

"1961 New York Yankee Yearbook"

"The World Champion Pittsburgh Pirates" Dick Groat 1961

"1960 The Last Pure Season" Kerry Keane 2000

Interviews / Correspondence

- Bill Mazeroski
- Rocky Nelson
- Dick Groat
- Dick Schofield
- Hal Smith
- Bill Virdon
- ElRoy Face
- Bob Oldis
- Vernon Law
- Bob Skinner
- Bob Friend
- Gino Cimoli
- Clem Labine